# Mary and Your Everyday Life

## A Book of Meditations

**Bernard Häring, C.SS.R.**

**LIGUORI**
PUBLICATIONS

One Liguori Drive
Liguori, Missouri 63057
(314) 464-2500

Published originally in Italian
as *Un Mese Mariano*
in April 1977
Simultaneous English translation
for England and
the British Commonwealth
by St. Paul Publications
Slough/England

Imprimi Potest:
Edmund T. Langton, C.SS.R.
Provincial, St. Louis Province
Redemptorist Fathers

Imprimatur:
+ John N. Wurm
Vicar General of St. Louis

ISBN 0-89243-070-2
Copyright © 1978, Liguori Publications
Printed in U.S.A.

Library of Congress Catalog Card Number: 77-92897

### Acknowledgment

My gratitude to Sister Joyce Gadoua and Miss
Phyllis LeVoie not only for typing and retyping
the pages of this English manuscript but also
for their competent help in correct English
usage.

Bernard Häring, C.SS.R.

"The souls of the just are in the Hand of God, and no torment shall touch them."

## Catherine E. Rosebrough
### Nov. 21, 1912
### Sept. 24, 1987

"Happy are those who have died in the Lord; let them rest from their labors for their good deeds go with them."

Lord Jesus, Our Redeemer. it is in Your Death that we find our salvation. And, by Your Mercy, all who live in Faith find Peace!

Welcome now, into Your Presence, Your departed Servant, — there to find Eternal Rest and Peace! We ask this through the same Christ, Our Lord. Amen.

I am the
*WAY*, the
*TRUTH*,
and the
*LIFE.*

John 14:6

784-5  ESPAÑA  © J.B. Co.

# Table of Contents

*Introduction*

The Second Vatican Council has crowned the *Dogmatic Constitution on the Church* with a beautiful chapter on Mary, the prototype and model of the Church. The Church cannot come to a full understanding of her union with Christ and her service to his Gospel without a profound love and knowledge of Mary, the Mother of our Lord and ourselves. Unfortunately, after the Council, many people of the Church did not give proper attention to this chapter.

Our veneration and love of Mary must not be minimized or de-emphasized, but rather, renewed and deepened. Too much attention to private revelations and doubtful apparitions of the Blessed Virgin neither help the cause for Christian unity nor our own love of Jesus. Therefore, we turn our attention in these meditations primarily to Holy Scripture and the liturgy.

We venerate in Mary, the queen of the prophets and apostles, the courageous woman, the humble handmaid of God and men, the one who lives fully the new law of the beatitudes. Through all that she is and tells us, she leads us to Christ.

If our veneration of Mary is authentic, then we can hope for a new springtime of evangelization and progress in the cause of Christian unity.

1

Mary, Sign of Hope

In the midst of a male-centered culture that looked down upon women, the first pages of Holy Scripture underline the equal dignity of woman and man. "Then God said, 'Let us make the human person in our image, after our likeness. . . .' God created the human person in his image, in the image of God. Male and female he created them" (Gn 1:26-27). Both woman and man have this great mission to be an image of God for each other: an image of his fidelity, his goodness, his tender love. We can only cry for pain seeing that both betrayed their dignity instead of receiving each other as a gift of God and praising him together. They become self-centered and conceal God more than they reveal him.

Yet, God's promise is with them from the beginning. There will come a new Adam and a new Eve. The woman is a sign of hope: "The Lord God said to the serpent: 'I will put enmity between you and the woman, between your seed and her seed; he shall bruise your head, and you shall bruise his heel' " (Gn 3:14-15).

The victor over arrogant and evil spirits will be Jesus Christ, the new Adam; but the promise of the Savior is introduced by the image of the humble and courageous woman who is set as a sign against the evil one, against all those who in their arrogance and pride refuse to adore God and will not love their fellow-man. God promises the woman who will be a true image of God that her offspring will manifest all the goodness and faithfulness of God. He will be the visible image of the invisible God and the new Eve will be his companion in her humility and purity.

In a time of great distress, the prophet Isaiah, inspired by the Spirit of God, invites the king of Judah to ask for a sign that God will set his people free. However, the king refuses to believe and to pray for a sign. And yet, God promises through his prophet: "The Lord God himself will give you a sign. Behold, a virgin shall conceive and bear a son and she shall call his name Emmanuel" (Is 7:14). In Israel, it was the right of the father to give to the son a name. It is an astounding privilege that a woman will give to the promised Savior the name Emmanuel, that is, God-with-us. God will be with her — "The Lord is with you." She will experience, in a unique way, the nearness of the Lord. All her being spells out for us: "The Lord is near."

Still referring to the great prophecy that perceives a virgin who will give birth to the One whom she will call Emmanuel, Isaiah offers the glorious vision of the future Redeemer: "To us a child is born, to us a Son is given; and the government will be upon his shoulder, and his name will be called Wonderful Counselor, Mighty God, Everlasting Father, Prince of Peace . . . and of his reign and of his peace there will be no end" (Is 9:5-6).

We can hardly doubt that in the family of Mary these promises were frequently meditated upon, and that, together, they sang the great songs of Second Isaiah on the servant of Yahweh theme. As the virgin was for centuries a sign of God's promise to his people, so Mary, under the guidance of the Holy Spirit, lived the hope and expectation of Israel. Her whole life becomes a fervent prayer for the longed-for advent: "Shower, O heavens, from above and let the skies rain down righteousness; let the earth open that salvation may sprout forth, and let it cause righteousness to spring up also. I, the Lord, have created it" (Is 45:8). Before Mary received the message of the angel that she was the chosen one, she, the fairest daughter of Sion, prayed daily that the womb of the promised woman might open and salvation might spring forth. The Lord's promise and blessing were with her before she could know that she was the chosen one to give the wonderful name to the Messiah, "Emmanuel," "God-with-us."

Mary surely lived most intensely the charism of the virgin who lives fully in vigilant waiting for the coming of the Lord. Saint John, whom Jesus entrusted to Mary and Mary to him, is the embodiment of the special charism of the virgin. He is "the man waiting for the coming of the Lord" (cf. Jn 21:20-23). This charism is given in the highest way to Mary. The oil in her lamp is burning; all her being longs for the Lord in readiness to greet him when he comes.

If we want to truly venerate Mary, the great sign of the promise, the new Eve, then we should above all appreciate the charism of vigilance and readiness. As men and women complement each other (mutually making up what is lacking in each), they should follow the new Adam and the new Eve, trying to become ever more fully an image and likeness of God, making visible for each other the presence of God: "God-with-us."

The Lord comes day by day through so many gifts and in the needs of our fellow-men. He calls us and urges us to be with him and to honor his coming. Blessed are we if we follow Mary in her *vigilance and readiness.*

We praise you, God almighty Father,
for having given to your people
  and to all of humankind the virgin,
a great sign of hope
  for the coming of the One
who will make you
  fully visible to us —
  the Emmanuel.

We pray that daily we may live with Mary,
hope in gratitude,
and ever be vigilant
   in the readiness to respond
with all our being
to your calling and your gracious coming.

O Mary, whenever we remember you
   and call upon your name,
we feel hope in us and long to know
   with you the Emmanuel —
   the experience of God's nearness.
We thank you for your fervent prayer,
   for your longing that was fulfilled
in the coming of our Savior.
Pray for us, that our lives
   may be a constant thanksgiving
   for his coming and become for many
a sign of hope, of trust,
and an invitation to seek the Lord. Amen.

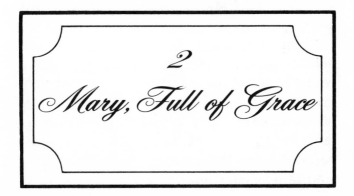

*2*

*Mary, Full of Grace*

"The angel Gabriel was sent from God to a town in Galilee called Nazareth, with a message for a virgin betrothed to a man named Joseph, a descendant of David. The girl's name was Mary. The angel went in and said to her,

'Greetings, most favored one, the Lord is with you.' But she was deeply troubled by what he said and wondered what this greeting might mean. Then the angel said to her, 'Do not be afraid, Mary, for God has been gracious to you; you shall conceive and bear a son and you shall give him the name Jesus' '' (Lk 1:26-31).

The fullness of time has come. The sign of the promise, the virgin, is now manifest to us; we know her name: Mary. Hers is the privileged name of God's design, a name that fills our heart with trust and joy.

With God's angel we say "Greetings to you." (This is the way we speak to her in our "Hail Mary"; we might also translate the word as "Rejoice.") God himself invites Mary to rejoice for the coming of the Messianic era. How could she not rejoice knowing that she is the promised sign that announces the coming of the Prince of Peace. Whenever we greet her with the "Hail Mary," we join her in her joy and gratitude.

"Full of grace," so God has graced her. She belongs totally to the Servant of Yahweh of whom the Lord spoke by the prophet: "Behold my servant, whom I uphold, my chosen one on whom my favor rests" (Is 42:1). She has found favor before the Lord in view of him who is the beloved Son. The greeting that comes from God is a mighty word; we may say it is an effective sacramental sign. God showers the heart of Mary with Messianic joy; she is the first to foretaste the coming of the Messianic age. Through a special revelation Mary comes to know that she is a sign of hope, a sign that God fulfills his promises to Israel. Her whole life sings of God's faithfulness: "Firm in his promise to our forefathers, he has not forgotten to show mercy to Abraham and his children's children forever" (Lk 1:55). From beginning to end, the life of Mary is graced; for she renders thanks always and everywhere, and thus she is open to experience the Lord's graciousness and to respond with generosity and ever greater gratitude.

Grace (*charis*) is not a thing; it is God's attractive love: God himself turning his countenance to us, manifesting his love to us in order to draw us to his heart. And no other person who lived prior to Mary has ever been so closely drawn to the heart of God as she. Since her earliest youth, meditating upon the great Messianic prophecies and all the events of salvation history, each word spoke to her of the attractive love of the Lord.

"The Lord is with you." Now the great moment of history has come when the virgin will learn and understand in a unique way the name "Emmanuel," "God-with-us." The Lord is with her and she who is the daughter of Israel, the promised to all nations, does not think only about herself. Rejoicing in the presence of the Savior, she calls him God with *us*, in view of *all* of us. Her joy in the presence of the Savior is our joy, and we join her in her praise and thanksgiving.

"Be not be afraid, Mary." The experience of God's presence and the revelation that the moment of fulfillment of the ancient promises had come shook Mary's whole being. In her humility, she would not have allowed herself to think that she would be the promised virgin.

Now God reveals himself and his designs to Mary. Her heart overflows with joy, and yet, she is shaken by her holy fear of God. This is the decisive moment in which Mary finds, on an even deeper level, the already existing mixture of joy and awe, of rejoicing in the Lord's nearness and of praising his holy name.

Our own spiritual life cannot be healthy without the contrast and harmony of these two poles of *joy and holy fear.* In Mary, the fear of God cannot be that of an unwilling slave, but the fear of the daughter of God. And yet, surprised by the newness of the revelation, she needed a special help from God to overcome all fear and entrust herself totally to him, that she could really touch the grace she had found before him. From beginning to end, she remains in the Lord's grace, for she is forever humble, grateful, and faithful.

**We praise you, Father,**
  **Lord of heaven and earth,**
**for what remains hidden**
  **to the wise and arrogant**
**you have revealed**
  **to the humble handmaid Mary,**
  **the daughter of Sion.**
**You have chosen her**
  **to be the queen of the prophets,**
**and all this you have done for us.**
**Grant that we always may praise your name**
**by the veneration**
**of the one you have chosen to be the Mother**
**of your only begotten Son made man.**

By the intercession of Mary,
and in the name of Jesus, the Emmanuel,
we pray
   that we too may experience his presence
   and come to know his name,
     "God-with-us,"
and rejoice in him
  who is the great sacrament
  of your nearness to us.

O Mary, what a joy it is
  that we can greet you
with the words, "full of grace"!
The favor you have found is for all of us;
the Lord who is with you
  comes to be with all of us.
We shall experience it if, like you,
  we are grateful and faithful.
Pray for us
that we may always be able to rejoice
  in the Lord's presence. Amen.

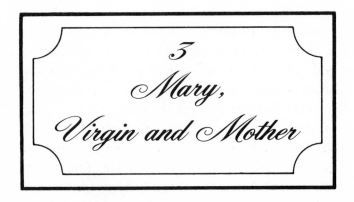

*3*

*Mary,
Virgin and Mother*

"You shall conceive and bear a son, and you
shall give him the name Jesus." The revelation
is clear. Mary cannot doubt that she is the sign

that is promised: the virgin who calls her Son, Emmanuel, "God-with-us."

Mary, the most humble among the humble, the holiest among all the saints, believes with the humble ones of the countryside that the promised Messiah will be the "Servant of God"; and through special revelation and grace, she comes to know the great mystery: the One whom she will call Jesus ("God our Savior") is the Son of the Most High and his reign will have no end.

She is the mother privileged to give him the name, a name which she experiences within her being. As mother, she will sing the praise of the Servant of God. As mother, she will give him loving care, and as believer, she will adore him.

Mary, the new Eve, the daughter of Sion, shares with her people a memory filled with gratitude for the wonderful things God has done for Abraham, Isaac, Jacob, David and all his descendants. The memory now becomes total celebration of gratitude for all that the Lord has already done and promised and now brought to fulfillment in her Son, who will reign in the house of Jacob and become the Savior and Lord of all the world. Each word of the angel is inspired by the Messianic prophecies of the Old Testament, and the memory and heart of Mary were filled by these prophecies which she had meditated upon so frequently with her family and friends, and in solitude. The promises resound in her heart all the time.

Now, through the special grace of the Holy Spirit, all that has transpired reaches its summit. What has happened becomes for her, and through her, God's self-bestowal on humanity.

She gives herself totally to him who is so gracious.

Mary is immaculate. She has not, like us, the need of ongoing purification. Her life, marked by the law of growth, is more than that of others. Her faith becomes an ever more glorious light. In her openness to the divine message and the gift of herself, she becomes ever more intensely grateful and joyous. The Lord God has guided her, step by step, to the moment in which she conceives the Son of the Most High. His grace has prepared her heart, soul, body, will and emotional response. Prepared is her faith so that her response and gift of self are fullness of joy.

Unlike Zechariah, Mary has no doubts that the revelation will be fulfilled. Yet, she humbly asks what her cooperation in this wonderful event will be: "How will this happen? I am still a virgin" (Lk 1:34). It is the prayer of the one who, like all of us, lives in faith, but with a fullness and sincerity that makes her the model of the Church. She teaches us how to search for nothing other than to know and to do the will of God.

Mary, although betrothed to Joseph, knew deep in her heart that she was not destined for a conjugal love as we understand that term. This is, at least, suggested by the sacred text. We do not know whether she had made a vow of virginity, or simply received an intuition that virginity would be the road which, for her, would be the sign and promise. But one thing *is* clear: Mary is *total openness to the will of God.* She anticipates, in faith, the prayer of her Son: "Thy will be done." In that total gift of self it becomes clear to her, in mind and faith, that she is, in a total and permanent sense, the virgin who will call her Son Jesus (God our Savior) and Emmanuel (God-with-us).

We thank you, God our Father,
that through Holy Scripture
  and the faith of the Church,
you have revealed to us that Jesus,
whom you have given to us as our Brother,
is the only One who has the birthright
  to call you Father,
having no Father on earth.
We praise your wondrous ways
by which you have prepared and guided Mary
for her faithful and grateful acceptance
  of your revelation
that she would be mother and virgin,
Mother of your only begotten Son.

O Mary, virgin and mother,
Mother of the Son of God made man in you,
and our mother also,
pray for us that like you
we might seek only one thing:
  the will of God,
that we might seek it
  with that humility and purity of heart
that distinguishes your faith. Amen.

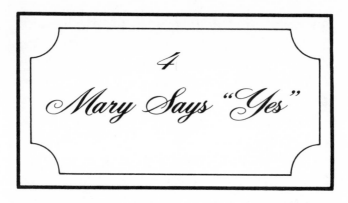

# 4
# Mary Says "Yes"

The prophecies that are now to be fulfilled echoed in the heart of Mary. "Comfort my people," says our God. "Speak tenderly to Jerusalem and cry to her that her time of slavery is ended. . . . A voice cries: In the wilderness, prepare the way of the Lord! Make straight in the desert a highway for our God. Every valley shall be lifted up, and every mountain and hill be made low; the uneven ground shall become level and the rough places, a plain. Hence, the glory of the Lord shall be revealed, and all people shall see it together; for the mouth of the Lord has spoken" (Is 40:1-5).

Now the hour has come, the hour to which the patriarchs and the prophets had looked. The fulfillment is greater than they could imagine. The angel says clearly how it will come to pass: "The Holy Spirit will come upon you and the power of the Most High will overshadow you; and for that reason, the Holy Child to be born will be called 'Son of God' " (Lk 1:35). This is the moment of a new creation by a wonderful intervention of the Holy Spirit. This is not the natural course of creation but a new manifestation of the power of the Most

High, a manifestation greater than the creation of the universe from nothingness. This is the moment to which the earth can respond only with silence, adoration, and everlasting thanksgiving.

To confirm the message for Mary, whose faith is already pure and strong, and to enhance our own faith the angel adds the message: "Moreover, your kinswoman Elizabeth has herself conceived a son in her old age; and she who is reputed barren is now in her sixth month, for God's promises can never fail." And yet, the miraculous fecundity of Elizabeth is only a small event in comparison to the unique newness which calls forth Mary's faithful and humble yes. "Here am I," said Mary. "I am the Lord's servant; as you have spoken, so be it." It is clear to the faith of Mary, and to our own, that she is the companion of Christ, the Servant of God. As the new Eve, she gives her *free and grateful assent* — "Here am I." Thus Mary, the humble handmaid, fulfills the life and the prayer of all the prophets: "Here I am, Lord, call me; here I am, send me."

Mary's unreserved gift of herself, her "yes" of faith and fidelity, is accompanied by the revelation of God's power. "So the word became flesh. He came to dwell among us, and we saw his glory, such glory as befits the Father's only Son, full of grace and truth" (Jn 1:14).

**We adore you, almighty God and Father,
for in your great love
    you have wrought miracles**

that no human mind ever
has thought possible
    or would have dared to hope.
Sending us your only begotten Son,
    you have given us
everything you could give us.
In him you reveal all your wisdom,
    your goodness, your gentleness and love.
We adore the One "conceived by the power
    of the Holy Spirit"
and born of the virgin
as "light of light, true God of true God."
You have given him to us as our Redeemer,
as the Man for all men, and as our Lord.
We give you thanks
    in the hope that we will be admitted
    to everlasting thanksgiving
in Jesus Christ,
    with Mary and all the saints.


O Mary, Mother of our Lord Jesus Christ,
we thank you for your humble "yes."
You did not want to be anything other
    than a servant of God,
following him who is the Servant of God
    and of all men.
We rejoice with you,
for the Most High has given you
    the honor and the joy
to be the Mother of his Son
    since he has taken flesh in you.
In our name, too,
    you have given the response of faith.
Pray that we too may respond
with all our heart,
    with all our being. Amen.

5

*Mary Visits Elizabeth*

For Mary, to know that her kinswoman in her old age has conceived a son is a sufficient invitation to serve her. Mary's prayer, "Behold the handmaid of the Lord," has, by necessity, a horizontal dimension. Simultaneously she is servant of God and his Gospel, and servant of her neighbor. We find Mary not only in the house of Zechariah and Elizabeth but also in Cana to help in household and kitchen. How many times must she have felt an invitation by the Lord's grace to serve those needing her?

As the servant of God, Mary meets Elizabeth and Zechariah. She comes to serve them, but at the same time she comes to bring them the message of joy and peace. "She went into Zechariah's house and greeted Elizabeth." Her greeting is more than a courtesy, or mere joy in the meeting of old friends. She, as the daughter of Sion, extends greetings with the age-old blessing and sign of hope: Shalom — peace. It is a blessing, and at this moment it is the fulfillment of the hope of Israel. She bears in her womb the Prince of Peace, who has taken our human condition to radiate joy and peace in the hearts of all people. He has come to establish a kingdom of peace and justice. Her coming and her greeting are signs of the coming and blessing of the Lord.

In our best tradition, the greeting among Christians was a praise of God and an exchange of the blessing toward each other. Perhaps we ourselves can rediscover the meaning of the meeting of Christians in our own homes and among friends. How beautiful was the ancient greeting "Praised be Jesus Christ," or, as it is spoken in all of the areas of Italy where Saint Alphonsus worked: "Praised be Jesus and Mary" — with the subsequent response — "Praised forever!" Why have we lost this beautiful tradition? Perhaps it had become too formal, too routine. We need to learn anew how to praise God and bless each other in a more spontaneous way when we meet. Even a simple "Good Morning!" can be a prayer and a blessing.

The Biblical text makes us consciously aware that Mary's greeting was a most powerful prayer and blessing. "And when Elizabeth heard Mary's greeting, the baby stirred in her womb." Through Mary, the one who is chosen to prepare the way of the Lord comes in contact with Jesus. His response is exultation, the sign of the peace and joy of the Messianic age.

As John is stirred by joy, Elizabeth herself is truly blessed by the greeting of Mary. "Then Elizabeth was filled with the Holy Spirit and cried aloud, 'God's blessing is on you above all women and his blessing is on the fruit of your womb.' " In that favored moment, Elizabeth received the Holy Spirit who inspired the prophets and made her discover the profound meaning of the visit of Mary. Her response is a blessing and a grateful affirmation of what God has done in Mary who is that great women in whom all generations will find the new Eve, who brings us the new Adam, Jesus Christ, the Savior of all. Each time we say the *Hail Mary,* we join the angel and Elizabeth in praise for all that God has done in Mary.

"Who am I that the Mother of my Lord should visit me?" Later, John the Baptizer humbly confesses that he is not even good enough to unfasten the shoes of Jesus. With astonishment he will ask, "Do you come to me? I need rather to be baptized by you" (Mt 8:14). With the same humility, Elizabeth wonders how it can happen that the Mother of her Lord comes to help her with the household. The coming of the servant of the Lord can be welcomed only with deep humility. The coming of Mary inspires veneration and awe, for blessed is he who comes in the name of the Lord.

In the house of visitation, we see a wonderful dialogue of faith, a shared prayer. There are five persons present: the eternal Word made man in the womb of the virgin; his Mother who brings the source of all blessing and peace; Elizabeth, filled with the Holy Spirit; and the greatest among all the prophets who prepares the coming of Christ, John the Baptizer. The fifth is Zechariah, a man of deep silence but with open eyes and heart. His silence is a true participation, listening and presence. The song he sings is: "Praise to the God of Israel."

Every Christian family and community is called to be a house of prayer and thus a source of joy for many. All of us will be helped to discover the signs of the times and to detect the presence of the Lord when we gratefully *share our faith and join in the praise of God.*

Lord Jesus Christ, we thank you
   with Elizabeth, John, and Zechariah
for your visit in their house;
we thank you for all the times
   you have visited us in our lives
and in our families.
We thank you, Father almighty,
for the coming of the greatest
   of all guests,
your only begotten Son made man for us.
He is your gift
but through your grace
   Mary is also a gift to us.
Grant to us that, like Mary,
we also may bring Jesus,
   his blessing and his peace
to our friends,
to everyone we meet.


We thank you, Mary, with all the people
to whose houses you have brought
   the blessing and peace of Christ.
Bless us with your greeting "Shalom,"
and pray for us that we may be attentive
to the many signs of the coming of Christ
   into our life. Amen.

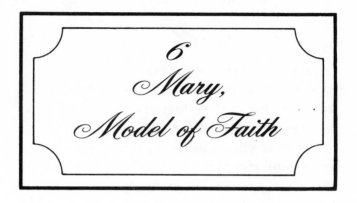

6
Mary,
Model of Faith

"How happy is she who has had faith that the Lord's promise would be fulfilled." We cannot offer any greater praise of Mary than that proclaimed by Elizabeth. Mary is the mother of the Church above all as a model of faith. Faith is joyous, grateful and humble acceptance of him who is the Way, the Truth and the Life.

Mary conceived in her womb the Incarnate Word of the Father when she received in her heart the good news of the coming of the Redeemer and the mission entrusted to her. Her faith response, "Here I am, the Lord's servant," is faith filled with trust and hope. Her faith is total surrender and trust in God which engender ongoing vigilance for the signs of God's will and bring forth love for the life of the world.

The faith of Mary is joy, but also a humble and eager searching for the will of God. In her faith, Mary can discern the signs of God's presence. She is a model for the Church as she combines gratitude for God's undeserved gift with readiness to be of service to others. All the wonderful things of which the Letter to the Hebrews speaks become an even greater song of joy when we think of the faith of Mary. "Faith gives assurance to our hopes, and makes us certain of realities we do not see. It is for their faith that the people of old stand on record. By faith, we perceive that the universe was fashioned by the word of God so that the visible came forth from the invisible" (Heb 11:1-3). In fullness of faith, Mary perceives the wondrous new creation that happens in the Incarnation of the eternal Word. It is the creation of the new earth and the new heaven, a creation more wonderful than that of the visible universe.

"Without faith, it is impossible to please God" (Heb 11:6). Mary pleases God more than any other creature because she excels by her faith and trust in God.

"By faith, Noah, divinely warned about the unseen future, took good heed and built an ark to save his household. Through his faith, he put the whole world in the wrong and made good his own claim to the righteousness which comes from faith" (Heb 11:7). Through faith, Mary becomes for us the ark of salvation through which the Savior of the world comes to us. She is the model and the promise for the Church which is the ark of salvation according to the measure of faith.

"By faith, Abraham obeyed the call to go out to a land destined for himself and his heirs, to leave home without knowing where he was to go" (Heb 11:8). By faith, Mary far surpasses the faith of Abraham and all the patriarchs as well. She is ready to leave all of the usual life patterns behind, setting out into a totally new and unknown land and accepting the mission to be the mother and deaconess, the servant of the Savior of the world. In faith-like obedience, she accepts the greatest exodus, that of Christ: the exodus beyond Egypt and the desert to that of the Cross.

"By faith, Abraham, when the test came, offered up Isaac: he had received the promises, and yet he was at the point of offering his only son" (Heb 1:17). God did not want Abraham to really sacrifice his son. Through a deepened and more illumined faith, God freed Abraham and his offspring from the pattern of his former culture where so frequently the first-born was sacrificed. God did not want Pilate and the people to kill his beloved Son, but he wanted Jesus, in whatever might happen, to make manifest his total readiness to give himself for the salvation of humankind. In his self-bestowal, he is totally followed by Mary, the deaconess of salvation. She joins, with a wounded but loving heart, the sacrifice of Christ on the Cross.

"And, what of ourselves? With all these witnesses to faith around us like a cloud, we must throw off every encumbrance, every sin to which we cling, and run with resolution the race for which we are entered, our eyes fixed on Jesus, on whom faith depends from start to finish" (Heb 12:1). Mary exceeds the faith of all people because her total being turns to Jesus; she knows him as the Savior of all and she gives herself totally to him who is the Servant.

It is in this way that Mary teaches all of us. In all that she does and says, she reminds us there is *no salvation in any other name save in that of Jesus.*

We praise you, Father,
  source of all life and light
for having sent us Jesus Christ, your Son,
Son of man, the Son of Mary.
We thank you for having given Mary
a faith so pure, so strong, so joyous
that she became
  the most privileged messenger of salvation
and the model of faith.
With Elizabeth and with the whole Church,
we praise the faith of Mary.
We praise you, the Giver of all good gifts,
and the Holy Spirit
  who prompts the faith in our hearts.
We thank you for the new ark of salvation,
the Church that becomes visible
as the community of believers in Mary,
  the model of faith.
With the whole Church we look to her,
  the most pure virgin,
who harmonizes so perfectly
  her faith and her life.
Trusting in her intercession we pray:
  Deepen our faith that each of us
      may be blessed on behalf of faith,
  and that we always may trust
    that your words will be fulfilled
  in all who put their faith in you.


O Mary, each time we pray,
  "Blessed are you among women,"

we praise you on behalf of your faith.
Pray for us that our faith
  may always be strong and radiant,
filled with hope and readiness
  to become, with you, a living gospel,
bringing the Messianic peace
  to all people. Amen.

7

*Mary's*
*Song of Praise*

"You, Israel, my servant, Jacob, whom I have chosen, the offspring of Abraham, my friend — you whom I took from the ends of the earth and called from its farthest corners, saying to you, 'You are my servant, I have chosen you and not cast you off. . . .' 'I will help you,' says the Lord; your redeemer is the holy One of Israel. . . . You shall rejoice in the Lord; in the holy One of Israel, you shall glory" (Is 41:8-16). This prophecy is fulfilled in Mary, the daughter of Sion, the crown of the history of Israel.

She is truly Israel, the servant, the humble handmaid who can sing the song of faith and joy, the song of the servant that will be fulfilled in Jesus, her Son.

If we meditate on the songs of the servant in Second Isaiah (42:1-4; 49:1-7; 50:4-11; 52:13—53:12), and then upon the Magnificat, we see the spiritual unity. Thus, Scripture tells us that Mary is the new Eve, Israel in its best, and she is truly on the side of the hoped for Messiah, the Servant of God.

Luke says with simplicity, "And Mary said." Surely Mary lived the song of the servant and shared it with Elizabeth and Zechariah. But it is not merely a song in one great peak experience. It is the word and prayer displayed so lavishly by the totality of her life, thoughts, desires, and actions. In the hours of joy and in the moments of suffering, and even under the Cross, Mary's life will sing the song of the servant. Mary *is* the Magnificat. The apostolic community finds in this great song of praise a perfect blend of the life and the role of Mary in the Church.

The Magnificat expresses more than just the personal faith of the Virgin and her most intimate union with God. It is the life-song of the one whom we rightly honor as our model and as the mother of the Church. Mary's life manifests what is meant to be the role of the Church throughout salvation history, enabling the Church to proclaim that God is on the side of the little ones. He it is who humbles the arrogant and exalts his Servant, Jesus Christ, and all those who follow him, after the example of Mary.

"Tell out my life, the greatness of the Lord." Since the Greek text allows for two translations, it is equally acceptable to say, "Tell out my soul, the greatness of the Lord." Surely it is the most intimate life in Mary that sings the song of the servant, but it is also her whole life. She is totally consecrated to the adoration and praise of God who manifests himself in the fullness of her being. Her life is thanksgiving. She is, with Jesus and in view of Jesus, the perfect Eucharistic person. As adorer of the Father "in spirit and truth," part of her thankful adoration is her sensitivity to the needs of others and her desire to bring the good news of salvation to all people, thus honoring and praising God.

"Rejoice, rejoice my spirit in God my Savior." We could also translate: "Rejoice, my spirit, in Jesus," for the name Jesus (in Hebrew "Joshua") means literally "God my Savior." The spirit of Mary is touched and moved by the Holy Spirit. In her life is fulfilled the prophecy of Ezekiel: "I will put my spirit in you" (Ez 37:14), and again, "and I will put my spirit within and cause you to walk in my statutes and be careful to observe my law" (Ez 36:27).

The early Church Fathers called Mary "the spouse of the Holy Spirit," for she is total docility and receives the gifts of the Holy Spirit with the most profound gratitude. She is fullness of Messianic joy and the most privileged messenger of the gladdening news. Her faith is joy, and who truly comes in loving contact with Mary will experience the same *joy of faith*.

**We praise you, Father almighty,
for in Mary you have given us**

the new Eve, the strong woman,
a sign of the new heaven and the new earth.
We praise you for having given Mary
   that fullness of faith's joy
from which flows the strength to serve you
   in all things.
We pray in the name of Jesus your Servant
followed by Mary the humble handmaid:
   Let our whole life become
      an ongoing song of your greatness,
   your holiness and mercy.
   Grant to us a heart renewed,
   cleanse us by the grace
      of the Holy Spirit
   that we may always rejoice in you,
      almighty Father,
   and in Jesus Christ our Savior.


Thank you, O Mary,
thank you, for you have sung and lived
   the song of the servant,
the hymn of joy, in our name as well.
You have prayed for us
that we may join you in the praise
   of God's greatness
and in the joy of being near to him.
And so we say "thank you"
   together with all the saints
who in the new heaven and
   on the new earth
sing with you the praise
   of the Lord. Amen.

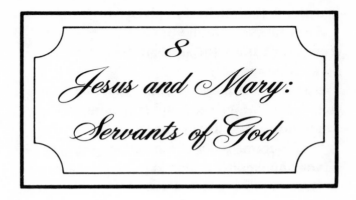

8

*Jesus and Mary:*

*Servants of God*

"Listen to me, O coastlands, and hearken you people from afar. The Lord has called me from the womb of my mother; he called me by name. . . . He said to me, 'You are my servant, Israel, in whom I will be glorified. . . .' And now the Lord who formed me from the womb calls me to be his servant, to bring Jacob back to him, and that Israel might be gathered to him, for I am honored in the eyes of the Lord, and my God has become my strength. He says, 'It is too light a thing that you should be my servant to raise up the tribes of Jacob and to restore the remnant of Israel; I will make you a light to the nations, that my salvation may reach to the ends of the earth'' (Is 49:1-6).

In the Magnificat, Mary shares with the Church her knowledge of the name of the Messiah, ''the Servant of God,'' that the people of God may also come to know it ever more fully. She is worthy to sing the song of the Servant, for she herself is totally a servant of God and men. In her life's song, the Virgin proclaims the name of Jesus and makes him known as the light for the nations and the salvation for all the earth.

What remains hidden to the wise and arrogant God has revealed to his humble servant, Mary: the mystery of the kingdom that is proclaimed and brought into being by Jesus, the Servant. With great exultation, Jesus himself shares this truth with his disciples: "At that favored moment, Jesus exulted in the Holy Spirit and said, 'I thank you, Father, Lord of heaven and earth, for what remains hidden to the wise and learned you have revealed to the simple. Yes, Father, such was your choice. Everything is entrusted to me by my Father. Nobody knows who the Son is but the Father and who the Father is but the Son — and those to whom the Son may choose to reveal him' " (Lk 10:21-22). I think we can rightly assume that in this great moment Jesus was thinking of Mary together with all who follow her in the path of humility. Nobody comes closer to the mystery of the Servant than Mary; for she, the humble handmaid, knows that everything is a gift. "So tenderly he has looked upon his servant, humble as she is. For from this day forth, all generations will count me blessed, so wonderfully has the Lord, the mighty One, dealt with me." She is blessed and worthy to be praised for she is a servant, immaculate, totally free from the stain of arrogance, from all desire to make herself the center of attraction. Those who turn truly to Mary — and come to know her — will, with her, turn totally to Christ and will learn to know and to honor Jesus, the total Servant.

Mary is a spotless mirror, faithfully reflecting the grace of God. Therefore, we praise the Lord over and again in calling her blessed among women. However, our praise is truly adoration of God, the Father, if the humility of Mary, who follows Christ the Servant, becomes the program and purpose of our whole lives. When we truly come to know and to love Mary, we will ask her to pray that the same *gift of humility* may be granted to and received by us so that the mystery of the kingdom of God can be revealed to us and through us.

**We praise you, Father,**
   **Lord of heaven and earth,**
**for having revealed the name of Jesus,**
   **the name Emmanuel,**
**and his name "Israel the Servant"**
**to your humble handmaid, Mary,**
**from the time you called him**
   **in the womb of his mother.**
**We thank you, Holy Spirit,**
   **for having inspired the life-song of Mary**
**and for assisting the infant Church**
   **to understand it;**
**for it is a light for our own life,**
   **a source of joy for all.**
**Come, Holy Spirit, and cleanse us**
   **from all arrogance and pride.**
**Grant that we not desire anything more**
**than to know the Father**
   **and the One he has sent, Jesus Christ.**
**For that reason we also pray**
   **for the gift of humility;**

help us that we always may be on the side
   of Jesus, the Servant,
by being on the side of the downtrodden,
on the side of the humble,
to whom you reveal
the name of the Father and of his Son,
   Jesus Christ.

We thank you, O Mary,
for your song of humility and joy.
Pray for us that we may fully be converted
to Jesus Christ,
   the Servant of God and men,
and thus be able to sing with you
   the song of joy
before Jesus, the Emmanuel. Amen.

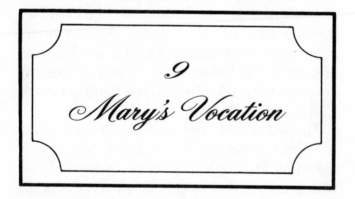

# 9
# Mary's Vocation

"Sing for joy, O heavens, and exult, O earth.
Break forth, O mountains, into singing, for the
Lord has comforted his people and will have
compassion on his afflicted. . . . Can a woman
forget her suckling child, that she should have
no compassion on the son of her womb? Even
though she may forget, yet I will not forget you.
Behold, I have graven you on the palms of my
hands. Lift up your eyes round about and see;

they all gather, they come to you. As I live, says the Lord, you shall put them all on as an ornament, you shall bind them on as a bride does'' (Is 49:13-18).

"Wonderfully has he dealt with me, the Lord, the mighty One." In her boundless gratitude, Mary, whose whole life praises the greatness of God, is able to discover his wonderful works done in and for her, and for all of humanity. Only a lack of humility can prevent the discovery of all the wonderful things God has done.

Mary has received the greatest sign of love and the greatest vocation that could ever be bestowed upon a mere creature. She is full of grace, strong in faith, and Mother of the Lord. A new creation, she is the new Eve because, through her, the new Adam, Jesus Christ, comes to us. She is more than the first Eve, the mother of the living; God gathers his people around her to make them all one family in Jesus Christ.

Through a profound love of Mary, who herself sings of her joy and gratitude throughout her whole life, we learn to have a memory filled with gratitude and to gain an awareness of all the wonderful gifts God has bestowed upon us. We discover our unique name with which each of us is called by almighty God. We come to a living faith in our vocation to holiness, a call to the ministry of unity and peace. Whoever gratefully discovers all the gifts of God in himself will be equally able to discover the inner resources of others. We shall give credence and trust to our neighbor; and together we will become more conscious that a divine artist, the

Holy Spirit, is present in the midst of people if for no lesser purpose than to make them masterpieces of his love and wisdom.

To refuse to see the good that God has so wonderfully done in us is a great sin against God, against oneself, and against one's fellow-man. From this blindness of ungrateful people arise flight from responsibility and escape from reality — the sin of those who always live with "if only." Things are quite different when we learn to sing with Mary for joy and gratitude; in so doing, we also find courage and joy in responding to God's call: "Here am I, Lord, call me, send me."

The world around us as well as our own lives become much more human and blessed in learning to *count the blessings* of the Lord and in sharing in the praises of his goodness. The consequence is that we discover thousands of wonderful things without wasting so much time recalling existing evils.

We praise you, almighty Father,
for all the wondrous things you have done
    in Mary, your humble servant.
As her children, we praise you
    for making her the mother of the living,
perfectly fashioned in Christ your Son
who has made himself freely
    the Servant of all people.
May we, with Mary,
    sing your wondrous deeds.
Make us gratefully remember
    all that you have given us.

Help us to discover the many signs
of the presence of your Spirit
that we may more gratefully
    and generously cooperate with his grace
and become, evermore,
    an image of your goodness
and your compassionate love.

O Mary, we thank you for your life
    and your word
which teach us gratitude,
which help us to discover
    all the wondrous things
    God has done for us
to the praise of his name,
and which prepare us to cooperate
    with his gracious calling. Amen.

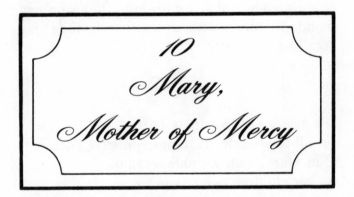

10

Mary,

Mother of Mercy

"And I will betroth you to me forever; I will betroth you to me in righteousness and in justice, in steadfast love, and in mercy. I will betroth you to me in faithfulness; and you shall know the Lord" (Hos 2:21-22).

In Mary, the new Eve, God glorifies his name, that is, his holiness and mercy. And

Mary accepts all the songs of Israel in the name of the new Israel, the universal People of God chosen from all the nations; she sings the praise of God who manifests his holiness by his mercy. She also proclaims that God — because of his holiness — rejects the arrogant, though his purpose is always to purify his people, to show healing forgiveness and to make them holy. Mary sees the promise of the Lord fulfilled: "My heart recoils within me, my compassion grows warm and tender. I will not give vent to my fierce anger, I will not destroy Ephraim; for I am God and not like a man, the holy one in your midst, and I will not come to destroy" (Hos 11:8-9).

"His name is holy, his mercy sure from generation to generation toward those who fear him." Mary's understanding of God was unforgettable. In the song of her life, there is a tension and harmony between the holy fear before all-holy God and trust in his compassionate love. Mary, who is sanctified by the holy God from the first moment of her life and who experiences God's sanctifying presence unto the end, is herself a great sign of the mercy of God who, for the sake of Jesus, has protected her from all contamination with the patterns of evil embedded in the society of her day. It is a sign of healthy religiosity if both religious experiences — fear of God and joyous trust in his mercy — are strong. Mary is the model of the Church, of all believers. The Church cannot be holy unless she constantly praises God's healing forgiveness and patience. Nor can she praise God's mercy toward her without showing compassion toward sinners, the poor and the outcasts. Where the Church follows Mary, her model, no one can be considered as hopeless. The very fear of God's holy name prevents this kind of rigorism.

Those legalists who sacrifice the human person for the letter of the law and who show no compassion for people of good will who find themselves in irregular situations do not know the holy name of God. The life and song of Mary are a commentary on the beatitude, "Blessed are the merciful, mercy will be shown them" (Mt 5:7). She is rightly praised as "the mother of mercy." She is the mother of the One who is mercy incarnate.

We are justified and sanctified by God's undeserved justice, by his mercy. None can live in the new justice without the readiness to follow Christ in his generosity and compassion. Jesus, the reconciler, is honored with Mary when *healing forgiveness is shown toward our fellow-men;* that is, when on all occasions people act as ambassadors of reconciliation and channels of peace. Thus united in the compassionate love of Christ, together, all can praise the holy name of God.

All-holy and all-merciful God,
grant that we may always honor your name
    in holy fear and joyous trust.
Let our whole life praise your mercy
    which you have shown to us
and which you also wish to manifest
    to others through us.
Give us the courage to face our misery

in deep faith that your holy love
  can heal us.
Make us gratefully remember
how often you have shown mercy to us,
and thus enable us to be ready
  to forgive our brothers and sisters,
not only seven times,
  but seventy-seven times seven.
Make of us a living gospel
  of your holiness and mercy.

Thank you, O Mary,
  Mother of Perpetual Help.
Your immaculate holiness and
  your absolute humility
are a great challenge to turn away
  from all pride and self-centeredness
and give the glory to God alone.
Thank you for comforting us
  by your song of God's mercy,
daring us to go to the house
  of our Father and say "Our Father."
Pray for us that all our life
  may express childlike trust
in the merciful Father of all.
May we never forget that
  though he is near,
God is a fathomless mystery
  who is infinitely beyond us.
Teach us that he is the holy One
  and we, creatures and sinners,
can come to him
  only because he manifests his holiness
through mercy. Amen.

## 11
## Mary's Humility

"The deeds his own right arm has done disclose his might; the arrogant of heart and mind he has put to rout; he has brought down monarchs from their thrones, but the humble have been lifted high." Here too, we see that Mary is inspired by the Old Testament's piety and profound vision of the history of salvation. "To God, I commit my cause. He gives rain upon the earth and sends water upon the fields. He sets on high those who are lowly, and those who mourn are lifted to safety. He frustrates the devices of the crafty, so that their hands achieve no success. He catches the wise in their own craftiness, and the schemes of the wily are brought to a quick end" (Jb 5:8-13).

Our Lady of the Magnificat shows how false is an individualized religion. Mary is not in sympathy with those who think only of personal salvation and individual spiritual comfort. She is the companion of the Redeemer of the world. She discerns the profound meaning of the history of salvation. She sees the conflict between the Servant of God who honors the all-holy, all-merciful God and the dragon, the arrogant spirit which manifests itself in overpowering people through misuse of authority and exploitation of the weak and the poor.

As nobody else, Mary knows the conflict between two quite different Messianic expectations in the people of Israel. The priestly caste and the mighty of the land expect a powerful Messiah, a national hero, who can submit all other nations to the power of the Jews. Even the people of Nazareth and some of Mary's kindred, along with those who begin to follow Christ as disciples, are captives of these false expectations. On the contrary, Mary, from the very beginning sings, with all her life, the true expectation: the Servant of God, the Messiah whom the Father sends will put the arrogant to rout. He opens the road of salvation to us by his humility which is emulated by Mary, the humble deaconess who is to stand under his Cross.

Each of us should examine his own life history in the light of the Magnificat and especially in the light of the history of salvation in which Christ, the Servant, overcomes collective arrogance and pride. In this same perspective, the history of the Church should be studied. Visibly, she prospers and finds the assistance of God whenever she follows with Mary, the handmaid, Christ, the Servant. Through a spirit of humility and gentleness, the Church can draw all people to Christ. If with Mary and Joseph we sing the song of the Servant, we will always better understand the profound meaning of the history of salvation. Before our eyes should always stand Jesus who, with Mary and Joseph, lived his *daily life in humility*. It is the humble people who keep the world together; it is in them that Jesus continues to reveal himself.

When we listen to Mary's Magnificat, she differs greatly from the falsified pictures of inauthentic private revelations in which people believe that because our Lady appeared in traditional dress she thus passed judgment on the length of women's skirts! Mary is not a ritualist. She does not talk to people about minute details, but she continues through her life-song to speak to us on the great themes of salvation, on the humble exercise of authority, on concern for the common good, on justice and peace, and on respect for the weak and the oppressed.

We adore you, all-holy and almighty God,
for you have and will always put to rout
   the arrogant, the oppressive and the unjust.
You will always be on the side
   of the oppressed,
the lowly and the outcast.
We praise you, for you have exalted
   your humble Servant, Jesus Christ.
You have given him a name
   above all names;
and you have exalted Mary,
   the humble handmaid,
to be the Queen of heaven.
You have made her a mighty prophet.

O Mary, how great are you,
   how glorious, how wonderful;

**you have fully lived the mystery**
  **of salvation,**
  **uncontaminated by a lust for power.**
**Pray for us**
**that the Lord may keep us far from**
  **the temptation to arrogance,**
**vanity, and exploitation of others. Amen.**

## 12
## Mary's Gratitude

"Rise up in splendor, for your light has come and the glory of the Lord has risen upon you. . . . Nations shall come to your light and kings to the brightness of your rising. Lift up your eyes round about and see; they all gather together and come to you. Your sons shall come from far, and your daughters shall be carried in the arms. Then you shall see and be radiant, your heart shall thrill and rejoice. . . . Your sun shall no more go down, nor your moon withdraw itself; for the Lord will be your everlasting light, and your days of mourning shall be ended. Your people shall all be righteous. The last one shall become the first and the smallest one a great nation. I am the Lord; in its time I will hasten it" (Is 60:1-21).

"The hungry he has satisfied with good things." The Magnificat is a song of joy and

gratitude for the fullness of God's graciousness
and fidelity revealed in the Messianic era. He
responds to humankind's hunger and thirst for
justice and salvation which his spirit has
awakened. Those, however, who boast in their
power and cling to their wealth cannot recognize the Servant of God; and, consequently,
they go empty-handed. Here again, the Magnificat closely resembles the formulations of
the beatitudes. "Blessed are those who hunger
and thirst for God's saving justice, they shall be
satisfied" (Mt 5:6). Mary is, with all her being,
in the song of her life, the great teacher of the
gift of salvation. Only those who honor God as
God and render thanks for everything can receive his grace. With Mary, we profess our
faith: "We believe in the Holy Spirit, the Lord,
the giver of life." God, in his superabundant
freedom and love wants to share with his creatures, his joy, goodness, and wisdom. But, God
is holy. He cannot give himself to those who, in
their arrogance, place themselves above him.

Mary praises God with her whole life. Her
spirit is filled with gratitude, and she is full of
grace. In her humility and thankfulness, she is
the model of the Church who, by her mission
and through the power of the Holy Spirit, hun-
gers and thirsts that God may be glorified by all
men and that all may experience salvation.
Mary, the Queen of the prophets, warns us,
however, against the terrible emptiness and
frustration of those who are ungrateful. Where
there is no gratitude, the gift is lost. The all-holy
God cannot share himself with those who are
unwilling to give him honor and to sing his
praises with Mary. Thus Mary leads us again to

a deep understanding of the first basic beatitude — that of the poor who stand before God fully recognizing that all things are his gifts and therefore we are to rejoice, sharing the gifts of the one God and Father with each other. Before us stands Christ, who, infinitely rich, made himself poor so that in him we may be capable of sharing in the richness of God. And, because he humbled himself in his great hunger and thirst to make us rich, the Father has glorified his name; he has given him the name above all other names.

We are called to nothing less than holiness. Through faith and Baptism, we are a new creation. We can live united with Christ. But for all this, what is indispensable is the unceasing prayer through which the Holy Spirit awakens in us an ever-increasing *desire for the fullness of holiness* — a desire to live with Mary in the discipleship of Christ's humility and purity of heart according to that undeserved gift of justification which we have received from God.

**We thank you, almighty and all-merciful God,**
**    that for our salvation**
**you have sent your eternal Word**
**to become like us in all things but sin.**
**You so graciously turned your countenance**
**to those who have hungered and thirsted**
**    to honor you, to love you,**
**and to sing the praises of your name.**
**We praise you for having revealed**
**    all your wisdom, might and glory**
**in your Servant, Jesus Christ,**

and also for having manifested
   your graciousness
   in your humble handmaid, Mary.
We pray in the name of your Servant
for the gift of humility and gratitude
that we may open our hearts
   to your goodness
and to the wealth of your love.
Free us from our selfishness,
   our tendency to become self-centered.
Dispel our empty pride.
Purify us by the fire of your love
so that the sufferings and difficulties
   of our lives
may become for us a process of learning
   to hunger and thirst
only for your saving justice.


O Mary, full of grace,
in your heart, the hunger and thirst
   of Israel and of all humanity
for salvation
   has come to fullness.
You who have experienced salvation,
pray for us that in humility, gratitude,
   and hunger and thirst
for God's saving justice,
we may prepare ourselves
   for the much desired grace
   of a holy life. Amen.

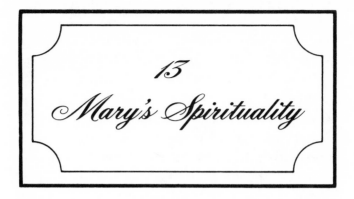

# 13
## Mary's Spirituality

"He has ranged himself at the side of Israel, his servant; firm in his promise to our forefathers, he has not forgotten to show mercy to Abraham and his children's children, forever." This again shows how deeply rooted in the Old Testament was Mary's spirituality. With great intensity, she lives the history of salvation. She surely had sung the great songs of the prophets long before she received the revelation that she was to be the virgin foretold by the prophets. "In that day, this song will be sung in the land of Judah: 'We have a strong city; he sets up salvation as walls and bulwarks. Open the gates that the righteous nation which keeps faith may enter in. You keep in perfect peace those who have put their trust in you. Trust in the Lord forever, for the Lord God is an everlasting rock. . . . They shall live, their bodies shall rise. O dwellers in the dust, awake and sing. . . . On that day — the pleasant vineyard, sing about it! I, the Lord, amidst your people, every moment, I water it' '' (Is 26:1-4, 19; 27:2-3).

It is Mary, the daughter of Sion, who sings the song of joy. The Word that has taken human nature in her is the great sign of God's faithfulness and mercy. But how could she not sing for joy and gratitude; in her, the great promises have been fulfilled! The One she bears as mother is the new Israel, the Servant, the Son of man, the only begotten Son of God. From all corners of the earth, he will gather disciples who, with him and his Mother Mary, can sing in gratitude the song of the new Israel. Those who, with Mary, follow the Servant of God and man will constantly experience God's mercy, his fidelity to his own name.

A key word of the Old Testament is "covenant." The Magnificat shows us that the spirituality of Mary is covenant morality. She does not simply live as a private person. She lives before God in full union with those who expected the Messiah before her and with those who in generations to come will praise the Lord with her. She teaches us how to celebrate and to live the Eucharist. She remembers gratefully all that God has done in the past, the promises he has made since the time of Abraham. In Mary, the history of Israel comes to full life as she anticipates the life of the new Israel, the Church. In Abraham, God has blessed his offspring. Blessed is Mary the woman promised at the beginning of the ages, for blessed is the fruit of her womb. Mary sings the song of Israel as the one who first experiences the fulfillment of the promises; and Mary, more than Abraham, becomes the *model of faith* for the new People of God.

After the words of the Magnificat, we read the prosaic note, "Mary stayed with her about three months and then returned home" (Lk 1:56). The evangelist wants to remind us that Mary, who so wonderfully sang the praise of God, representing the whole of history, is in the house of Elizabeth to serve in household and kitchen. She is, simultaneously, evangelist and handmaid. To this humble girl God has opened the horizons of the history of salvation.

Almighty and all-holy God,
  with Mary we praise your greatness.
Faithful to your own name as Father,
you have shown mercy to Israel
  and to all nations.
You have fulfilled your promises
  in love for Mary
through her Son, your Christ.
We pray for your people Israel
that they may be blessed
  and turn to Christ your Son.
You have given us
  the new and everlasting covenant.
Grant us the grace
  to live in gratitude and fidelity,
praising your faithfulness.


O Mary, we thank you for the Magnificat,
for the song of your life
which enchanted Elizabeth and Zechariah
and all who have met you.
We thank you that, in your life,

you have made visible the mercy
    and fidelity of God,
who has done such great things in you.
Pray for us that our gratitude may increase
and that we may evermore appreciate
    the gifts of God
so that our life, too, may become a song
praising God's mercy and fidelity. Amen.

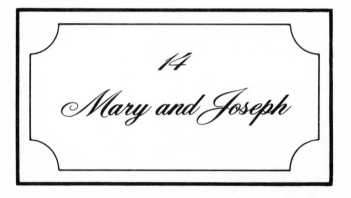

*14*

*Mary and Joseph*

"This is the story of the birth of the Messiah.
Mary, his Mother, was betrothed to Joseph;
before their marriage she found that she was
with child by the Holy Spirit. Being a man of
principle, and at the same time wanting to save
her from exposure, Joseph desired to have the
marriage contract set aside quietly. He had re-
solved on this when an angel of the Lord
appeared to him in a dream. 'Joseph, son of
David,' said the angel, 'do not be afraid to take
Mary home with you as your wife. It is by the
Holy Spirit that she has conceived this child.
She will bear a son; and you shall give him the
name Jesus (God is Savior), for he will save his
people from their sins.' All this happened in
order to fulfill what the Lord declared to the

prophet: 'The virgin will conceive and bear a son, and he shall be called Emmanuel,' a name which means 'God is with us.' Rising from sleep, Joseph did as the angel had directed him; he took Mary home to be his wife who without having intercourse with Joseph gave birth to her son. And he named the child Jesus" (Mt 1:18-25).

It is easy to discover the intention of this text of the Gospel of Matthew. The main purpose is to strongly affirm the virgin birth. Christ is born of the virgin Mary through the work of the Holy Spirit. He has only one Father, the Father in heaven. On the other hand, the Gospel exalts the role of the patriarch, Joseph. Matthew traces his lineage back to Abraham, our father in faith; the patriarch Joseph is presented as a man of unwavering faith and of great justice.

Joseph is a just man. To see that the virgin betrothed to him was pregnant must have caused him sleepless nights. And yet, he does not allow himself to utter suspicion or accusation. The decision he has worked out in his mind is not according to the written law or tradition but simply according to the law of love. In accord with the strict law, he would have had to hand a written declaration to the elders with the motives for his decision to repudiate Mary. This would have brought great pain to Mary. Feeling that he has no right to marry her, he finds a solution that would safeguard her reputation in a way that tradition could not. His anguish must have been as great as that of Abraham who thought he had to sacrifice his first-born son, Isaac. Like Abraham, Joseph receives a revelation from an angel of God, a revelation that opens up totally new horizons.

He knows from the Scriptures that the virgin will give the name to her Son, the name of Jesus. Now he is invited by God's angel to share in the privilege of the virgin, to experience the nearness of God in Jesus, the Savior. He is given to Mary and Jesus as companion and support for the joyous days and for the crucial hours.

In him, the history of the patriarchs which is a history of faith and exodus is lived again. We honor him with the name patriarch; for in him, who is just and strong in faith, is made visible the history of the patriarchs at its best. "By faith Abraham obeyed the call to go out to a new land destined for himself and his heirs; he left home without knowing where he was to go. By faith he settled as an alien in the land promised to him" (Heb 11:8-9). Joseph, too, accepts a mission that will lead him onto roads he does not yet know, but he will always walk in the way of faith; and for that, he will receive abundant light, more abundant than Abraham's. At Mary's side, Joseph, considered by law as the father of Jesus, will play an active role in the history of salvation. In his humility and faith, he will know with Mary the name of Jesus, Emmanuel, "God-with-us." With Mary he will serenade Jesus with the songs of the Servant by word and deed.

Joseph will live without earthly security. Arriving at Bethlehem, he will not find a home for Mary and her Son to be born; with Jesus and Mary he will live again the history of Israel as refugee people in Egypt. He will return to

Nazareth putting his trust in God alone. From a total lack of earthly security will come to him the experience of God who is our rock. He teaches us how to live in faith and hope with Mary and Jesus.

The Church of today lives anew that stunning exodus in the transition from one era to the next. Her people are losing many earthly securities while a number of human traditions are being shaken. In this situation, humankind can look to the Holy Family and learn that it is not imperative for Christians to seek earthly security but to *find strength in faith*. It is the purpose of the Church's life to manifest trust in the Lord, to live in his presence and know that God will abide in her. The Lord alone is her stronghold and he will be with the believers.

**We praise you, holy God,**
   **for having brought to fulfillment**
**the history of the patriarchs**
   **in Saint Joseph**
**whom you so graciously gave**
   **to Jesus and Mary**
**as companion and protector.**
**You have blessed him with a strong faith**
   **and great trust in you.**
**Through the intercession of Mary and Joseph,**
**we pray that you will always protect**
   **your Church**
**and bless her with the gifts**
   **of faith and trust.**
**Be with your Church, be with all of us**
**that we may not lose heart**

in these trying times of change,
indeed, of painful exodus.
May your Church live faithfully
   this period
as the major forces
   which influence human life
change and shift.
May she be a sign of fulfillment
   of the old promises
for Africa, and Asia,
   indeed, for all cultures.


Mary and Joseph, we thank you
for having lived the moments
   of uncertainty and anguish
with purity of heart, with one desire:
to be faithful to the Lord.
God's astounding plan made you seek
   new directions.
Though frustration was not spared you,
your faith was only strengthened.
Protect us by your intercession
that we may never forget
   the presence of our Lord
who is our joy and our strength. Amen.

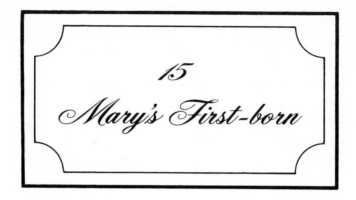

*15*

*Mary's First-born*

"In those days a decree was issued by the Emperor Augustus for a registration to be made throughout the Roman world. This was the first census of its kind; it took place when Quirinius was governor of Syria. For this purpose, everyone made his way to his own town. And so Joseph went from the town of Nazareth in Galilee to Judea, to register at the city of David, called Bethlehem — because he was of the House of David by descent; and with him went Mary who was betrothed to him. She was expecting a child, and while they were there, the time came for her baby to be born, and she gave birth to a son, her first-born. She wrapped him in his swaddling clothes and laid him in a manger, because there was no room for them to lodge in the house" (Lk 2:1-7).

The great moment awaited by the whole world has now arrived. And with the greatest intensity, Mary and Joseph live the exodus, the pilgrimage of Abraham, Isaac, Jacob and the patriarch Joseph, of Moses and of the whole people. They anticipate the history of the pilgrim Church on earth.

In extreme poverty, but with faith and trust and a great love as their true riches, Mary and Joseph live this breathtaking moment in the history of salvation. The external circumstances of Christ's birth should not lead us to consider this Child insignificant. This Infant is everything in all things, the greatest gift of the Father to his creation. He is the Child most wanted, most desired, most loved. And this Child lying in a manger is the Prince of Peace, the King of kings.

This great moment reveals to us a *true sense of poverty*. Mary and Joseph tell us one great truth: God alone suffices. What more could they desire than to know him whom God has called and whom they will call Jesus, Savior, Emmanuel, God-with-us?

Jesus is called the first-born of Mary. This does not mean that she gave birth to other children. But it does indicate that she who calls the only begotten Son of God her "first-born" knows that in the new family Jesus will have many brothers and sisters. He is the first-born of all creation; in him, the eternal Word of the Father, are created all things, and all things were made in view of him who came into the world as the light and life of the world. He is the first-born; the only One who has the full birthright to call the eternal almighty God his Father. He is the only begotten Son and yet, the first-born; for he wants to call us all to be his brothers and sisters and to join him in the cry of joy, "Abba, Father." It is in him that we can say, "Our Father." And it is also because of him that we have a right to call Mary our mother.

O all-holy God, we kneel
    in praise of your wisdom.
We adore you in the first-born of Mary,
    in your only begotten Son
in whom you have given us everything,
and in whom you have entitled us
    to call you our Father.
We praise you for you have manifested
    your fatherhood,
and the tenderness of your fatherly love,
giving us Jesus as our brother
    and Mary as our mother.
May all our life reflect your greatness,
and may our spirit rejoice in you
    and in the joy you gave us in Jesus Christ.
Make us grateful.
May your Holy Spirit come upon us
    so that our whole lives
may become thanksgiving, admiration,
    adoration, and praise of your name.


O Mary, how great must have been your joy
    in that moment.
Pangs of childbirth, the anguish
    of the exodus, the poverty of the stall
are only the background of your joy.
You do not have any other treasure
    but Jesus, your first-born;
and you have no other desire than
    to awaken trust in him
who is the Emmanuel, God-with-us,
    our salvation, our joy.

Pray for us
that we may obtain that poverty of spirit
   that allows us to find Jesus,
our only treasure,
our only love,
and to learn to love with him
   all for whom he came as Savior.
Pray for us that we may put all our trust
   in him. Amen.

*16*
*Mary, Mother
of the Good Shepherd*

"Now in this same district there were shepherds out in the fields, people keeping watch through the night over their flock. Suddenly, there stood before them an angel of the Lord, and the splendor of the Lord shone around them. They were terror-stricken, but the angel said, 'Do not be afraid! I have good news for you. There is great joy coming to the whole people. Today in the city of David a deliverer has been born to you — the Messiah, the Lord. And this is your sign: in a manger you will find a baby lying wrapped in his swaddling clothes.' All at once, there was with the angel a great company of the heavenly host, singing the praises of God: 'Glory to God in the highest, and on earth his peace for the people on whom his favor rests.'

"After the angels had left them and gone into heaven, the shepherds said to one another: 'Come, we must go straight to Bethlehem and see this event which the Lord has made known to us.' So they went with all speed and found their way to Mary and Joseph; and the baby was lying in the manger. When they saw him, they recounted what they had been told about this child; and all who heard were astonished at what the shepherds said. Mary treasured up all these things in her heart and pondered over them. Meanwhile the shepherds returned glorifying and praising God for what they had heard and seen; it had all happened as they had been told'' (Lk 2:8-20).

There is a profound meaning in the fact that God revealed Jesus, the Son of Mary, first to the shepherds through the song of the Messianic peace. This incident calls to mind two of the great Messianic promises on which Mary (and Joseph, too) had meditated throughout the years: that God himself would be the Good Shepherd, and that he would both be for us and bring to us the fullness of peace. With the visit of the shepherds who so fully joined them in the praise of the Lord and who became the first messengers of the coming of the Savior, great prophecies reechoed again in the hearts of Mary and Joseph: "Behold, the Lord God comes with might, with him is the rightful rule; behold his reward is with him, and his recompense before him. He will feed his flock like a shepherd, he will gather the lambs in his arms, he will carry them in his bosom, and gently lead those that are with young" (Is 40:10-11).

"Thus, says the Lord, God: behold, I myself will search for my sheep, and will seek them out. As a shepherd seeks out his flock when some of his sheep have been scattered abroad, so will I seek out my sheep; and I will rescue them from all places where they have been scattered on a day of clouds and thick darkness. And I will bring them out from the peoples and gather them from the countries, and will bring them into their own land; and I will feed them on the mountains of Israel, by the fountains, and in all the inhabited places of the country. I, myself, will be the shepherd of my sheep, I will seek the lost and I will bring back the strayed, and I will bind up the crippled, and I will strengthen the weak, and the sleek and the strong I will watch over; I will shepherd them in justice" (Ez 34:11-16).

Mary and Joseph have recognized in Jesus, God-with-us, the promised Good Shepherd who manifests to us the infinite love of God, our Father, who cares for his people. They rejoice in the simple shepherds who make Jesus known wherever they go. Mary and Joseph rejoice with the angels, for they know Jesus as the Prince of Peace.

More than anyone else, Mary knows that Jesus has not come to judge or to condemn but rather to seek the lost sheep and heal them. We have to see through the eyes of Mary and of the good shepherds in order to find Jesus, to rejoice with the angels, to sing his praise and proclaim his peace.

Mary treasures up in her heart the message brought by the shepherds and the angels. And her meditation on Jesus, the Prince of Peace, on Jesus the Good Shepherd, surely includes us — that the Church may never lack good shepherds shaped in the image of Christ, nor be without those who rejoice in the peace of Christ and share it with all people. When we celebrate these great events in the Eucharist, we should remember Mary gratefully. We need to be thankful for the message which is brought to us so that we can be fully open to the grace and joy of the Good News.

It is characteristic of Saint Luke, the great teacher of prayer, to terminate every great event with a choral ending in praise of God. Everywhere the shepherds proclaim the godly news, praising God. Mary is the model of the song of praise; a genuine veneration of Mary will lead us to *understand the Eucharist more fully*. It will transform all our life into a Magnificat, a praise of God for the good shepherds.

We thank you, almighty and all-holy God,
for in Jesus Christ you have fulfilled
   your promises
that you yourself would be the Shepherd
   of your people.
Make us holy, make us one in your love
   that we may better know Jesus,
the Good Shepherd,
and be always united with him.
Bless your Church, that she may always
   have good shepherds

who know how to praise you
   and how to bring the message of peace
to all people.
Create in us a great compassion
   for those lost
that we may, like Mary and Joseph,
know you as the Good Shepherd
and may make you known to all people
   of good will.

O Mary, Mother of the Good Shepherd,
pray for us and pray for the shepherds
   of the Church
that they may truly and fully know
   the name of Jesus,
the Good Shepherd.
Pray that their hearts,
filled with compassionate mercy
   for those who are astray,
may patiently seek them out and gently
   bring them home
into their Father's house.
Pray for us that gratitude may inspire
   all that we think,
desire, and do. Amen.

17

*Mary's*
*Part in the Covenant*

An important event in the life of Mary is the circumcision of Jesus, at which time his name is solemnly proclaimed, Jesus, "God our Savior." It is the moment in which the covenant of God with Abraham and Moses is proclaimed in the one who is simply, "the Covenant of the people."

"The Lord said to Abraham: 'I am God almighty; walk before me and be blameless. I will make a covenant between me and you and will multiply you exceedingly. . . . I will make nations of you, and kings shall come forth from you. I will establish my covenant between me and you and your descendants after you throughout their generations for an everlasting covenant, to be God to you and to your descendants after you. . . . I will be their God. . . . This is my covenant which you shall keep between me and you and your descendants after you: every male among you shall be circumcised. . . . This shall be a sign of the covenant between me and you. . . . He that is eight days old among you shall be circumcised' " (Gn 17:1-12).

For Mary and Joseph, the ritual of circumcision is a profound renewal of the commitment to the covenant and the law of the covenant which is above all: to love God with all our hearts, with all our souls, and with all our energies, and to love our neighbor as ourselves. The ritual is a memorial event when the Israelites gratefully recall all that God has done in the past.

For Jesus it is more than a remembrance of the past deeds of God. It is the fulfillment of the covenant God has promised to Abraham and his descendants; for with the coming of Jesus the new covenant begins.

"I am the Lord, I have called you in righteousness, I have taken you by the hand and kept you; I have given you as a covenant to the people, a light to the nations" (Is 42:6). This text is taken from the song of the servant which is so well-known to Mary. Her spiritual life is thoroughly nourished by these songs. Therefore, she knows with heart and mind that one of the great names of Jesus is "the Covenant of the people." Jesus is the man for all. He is incarnate solidarity (that is, incarnate source of unity, of our becoming *one people*) who thus establishes the law of saving solidarity (mutual active dependence and love) for all. Prepared in faith, Mary knows that she is not meant to live solely for her own salvation; living with Jesus who is the Covenant of the people, she is, therefore, thoroughly authorized to act as the deaconess of salvation.

All of Jesus' life is manifestation of the new covenant, but there are some solemn moments, one being the circumcision with the symbolic shedding of blood, the blood of the Covenant. Another profound moment is the baptism of Jesus in the Jordan during a general baptism. He hereby manifests that he is ready to bear the burden of all people, he who is the Covenant of mankind, the light for all nations and the Servant of God. As he commits himself publicly, the Holy Spirit comes visibly upon him and the Father proclaims him as his beloved Son. All this is merely a liturgical preparation for the great moment when Jesus, already baptized with the Holy Spirit, receives the real baptism in his blood, which is and will always be the blood of the new and everlasting covenant.

We celebrate our Baptism as sign of our insertion into the covenant. It becomes the full truth of our lives when we no longer live for ourselves but with Jesus, who is the Covenant, and with Mary, the deaconess of the Covenant, who help us to live for each other and bear one another's burdens. Each time we celebrate Baptism there is a spiritual presence of Mary who has lived, in a unique way, the transition from the Old to the New Testament. With Joseph she is the qualified witness to the circumcision of Jesus as a sign of continuity with the covenant God has made with Abraham.

In Baptism, solemnly, *we receive the honor and the name of children of God.* The name of Jesus was decided and even made known before he was conceived in the womb of his Mother, but it is the privilege of Mary and Joseph to confirm and proclaim his name. For us, the name of JESUS is always a prayer of praise and of petition: GOD, OUR SAVIOR. We put all our trust in him and thus praise his

name, and we bless each other in the name of
Jesus.

God of our fathers,
we praise you for the covenant
you have made with humankind
    from the beginning.
We glorify you for the covenant with Noah,
Abraham, Jacob, Moses,
    and with all your people;
for these covenants are the promise
of the One who is the abiding Covenant,
    Jesus Christ,
your only begotten Son whom you have sent
    to be our brother,
bearing our burdens
that we too may learn to bear the burdens
    of each other.
We thank you together with Mary
who has put all her trust in you
and who has, throughout all her life,
    honored the name of Jesus.
We thank you for the sign
    of the new covenant,
the Baptism that makes us
    sharers in the baptism
which Christ has received for us
in the Jordan and on the Cross.
During the baptism in the Jordan,
you have manifested him
    as your beloved Son,
and at our Baptism, you have assured us
that we can share in Christ's prayer
and can call you, "Abba," Father,

our Father.
Let this prayer, each time we say it,
be our expression of fidelity
    to the covenant,
and our gratitude for the blood
    of the new and everlasting covenant.


O Mary, how great must have been your joy
when, at the circumcision,
    you could proclaim the name of Jesus,
whom you recognized
    as the Covenant of the people.
Pray for us
    that we may better understand the meaning
    of the new and everlasting covenant
and thus come to live fully,
    in fraternal love,
the birthright which Baptism has given us.
    Amen.

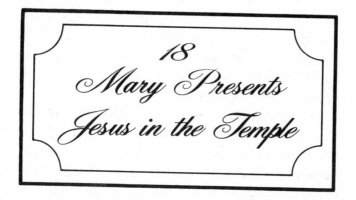

18
Mary Presents
Jesus in the Temple

"Then after their purification had been com-
pleted in accordance with the law of Moses,
they brought him up to Jerusalem to present
him to the Lord (as prescribed in the law of the
Lord: 'Every first-born male shall be deemed

to belong to the Lord'), and also to make the offering as stated in the law: 'a pair of turtledoves or two young pigeons' " (Lk 2:22-24).

The presentation of Jesus in the Temple was, like the circumcision, an act of obedience to the law of the old covenant, and thus at the same time, a prophetic gesture that announces the coming of the new covenant — that of the anointed one, Christ, the High Priest and Prophet.

God himself has, through Moses, explained the profound meaning of this act of presentation: "The Lord said to Moses, 'Consecrate to me all the first-born. Whoever is the first to open the womb before the people of Israel is mine. . . .' And when the Lord brings you into the land of the Canaanites as he swore to you and your fathers and shall give it to you, you shall set apart to the Lord all that first opens the womb. . . . And when in time to come, your son asks you, 'What does this mean?' you shall say to him, 'By the strength of his hand the Lord brought us out of Egypt from the house of bondage' " (Ex 13:1-14).

When Mary, in obedience to the law, fulfills this ritual praising God for the liberation from the bondage of slavery, she knows that Jesus belongs to God the Father in a unique way. The ritual is only a manifestation of the deepest truth that Jesus, from the beginning, is totally consecrated to the kingdom of the Father and to the Gospel. But, it becomes gradually clear to Mary that this road of Jesus will require detachment and great sacrifice on her part. At the proper moment she will humbly hide herself as John the Baptizer will do, so that Jesus, in his uniqueness, may be manifested to all as the prophet, the priest, and the sacrifice.

The presentation of the first-born is an act of consecration. While Mary fulfills this act, presenting the One who is consecrated by the Holy Spirit, she consecrates herself as his companion and servant. She knows that the ritual sacrifice of a pair of turtledoves cannot substitute for the offering of herself. This is so, especially in view of Christ who comes to offer himself.

At the baptism of Jesus in the Jordan, the dove becomes the symbol of the consecration through the Holy Spirit. Mary, with dove-like simplicity, is *always faithful and docile to the promptings of the Holy Spirit,* and thus fulfills her role in the work of redemption. Through the gifts of the Holy Spirit, she perceives what the Lord requests of her — here as she offers her first-born in the Temple and at every stage of her life.

We thank you, Lord God of history.
We thank you
   that through Moses, your servant,
you have revealed to us
   the profound meaning of the presentation
which came to its full truth
   in Jesus Christ,
the One who was expected by the prophets.
While Mary offered Jesus,
   she also presented herself
with the one great desire
   to honor your name in all things.

Grant through her intercession
that when we offer Jesus
   in the Eucharistic sacrifice
we may also offer ourselves wholeheartedly
   to your service with Jesus and Mary.

O Mary, present us with Jesus
   to the Father in heaven.
Pray for us that we may learn
   what a great joy it is
to know that we belong to God
   as his property,
consecrated to him
   together with your first-born, Jesus Christ.
   Amen.

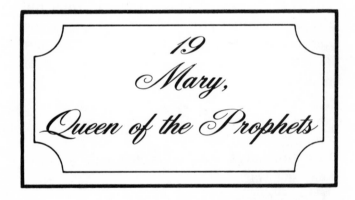

*19*

*Mary,*

*Queen of the Prophets*

"There was at that time in Jerusalem a man called Simeon. This man was upright and devout, one who watched and waited for the restoration of Israel, and the Holy Spirit was upon him. It had been disclosed to him by the Holy Spirit that he would not see death until he had seen the Lord's Messiah. Guided by the Spirit, he came into the Temple; and when the parents brought in the child Jesus to do for him what was customary under the law, he took him in his arms and praised God in these words: 'This day, Master, thou givest thy servant his discharge in peace; now thy promise is fulfilled for I have seen with my own eyes the deliverance that thou hast made ready in full view of all the nations: a light that will be a revelation to the heathen, and glory to the people, Israel.' The child's father and mother were full of wonder at what was being said about him. Simeon blessed them and said to Mary his mother, 'This child is destined to be a sign which men reject, and you too shall be pierced to the heart. Many in Israel will stand or fall because of him, and thus the secret thoughts of many will be laid bare.'

"There was also a prophetess, Anna, the daughter of Phanuel of the tribe of Asher. She was a very old woman who had lived seven years with her husband after she was first married, and then alone as a widow to the age of eighty-four. She never left the Temple but worshiped day and night, fasting and praying; coming up at that moment, she returned thanks to God; and she talked about the child to all who were looking for the liberation of Jerusalem" (Lk 2:25-38).

The Gospel of Luke presents Mary very clearly to us as the Queen of the prophets. When she brings her greeting and blessing to the house of Zechariah, John, still in the womb, leaps for joy and thus initiates his prophetic role of proclaiming the One who would baptize by the Holy Spirit. Elizabeth is filled with the Holy Spirit and, after a period of silence, Zechariah utters the great prophecy in a song similar to that of Mary.

When Mary brings Jesus to present him in the Temple another astonishing encounter with the prophets takes place. Two other noble representatives of the humble people of Israel encounter him at this time. The outpouring of the Holy Spirit upon Elizabeth and Zechariah, on Simeon and Anna is a sign of the new Messianic era. It becomes clear that God reveals himself to the humble and the simple. "I praise you, Father, Lord of heaven and earth, for hiding these things from the learned and wise, and revealing them to the simple. Yes, Father, such was thy choice" (Lk 10:21-22). Jesus will later refer to this scene: "Happy the eyes that see what you are seeing. I tell you, many prophets and kings wished to see what you now see, yet never saw it; to hear what you hear yet never heard it" (Lk 10:23-24).

Simeon and Anna are the privileged ones to whom God reveals the coming of the Messiah. Simeon and Anna are similar to Mary; they lived intensely the expectation and hope for the coming Savior. The encounter is occasion for the praise of the Lord; and the revelation granted to this holy group becomes, at once, proclamation of the things to come. Simeon announces Jesus not only as the liberator of Israel but also as the light of all nations, and Mary receives these prophetic voices of joyous praise and evangelization as the Queen of the evangelists and apostles. How she longs that all people may know the Savior!

Mary too receives a special prophecy, that of the sword of suffering. She is the one who is to follow Christ wherever he goes, even to the abyss of suffering. Mary and Joseph as well as

Simeon and Anna had meditated on the fourth psalm of the Servant of Yahweh: "He was despised and rejected by men, a man of sorrows and acquainted with grief. . . . Surely he has borne our grief and carried our sorrows" (Is 53:3-4).

From now on, the participation of Mary in the mystery of salvation comes to fuller light. More than the martyrs and the apostles, Mary shares in Christ's suffering. Because of her great love, her immaculate heart will suffer more than any other. It is from Christ, however, that her share in the work of redemption has its great fecundity.

Simeon leaves no doubt that, faced with Jesus Christ, *all men have to make their decision:* those who refuse to accept him as the Savior for the resurrection to life prepare their own downfall. The greatest pain for Jesus will be to see that some will resist and refuse salvation. This also is the sharpest sword that wounds the heart of Mary since, with Jesus, her Son and the Son of God, she is mother of all the living; and, as such, she desires nothing more than the salvation of all people.

**Heavenly Father,**
  **together with Mary and Joseph,**
**Elizabeth and Zechariah,**
  **John the Baptizer, Simeon and Anna,**
**we praise you for having sent us**
  **Jesus the Prophet.**
**We praise you for the outpouring**
  **of the prophetic spirit**

guiding your people in the hours
   of darkness.
We thank you for all the prophets
who have prepared the coming of Jesus,
   the Prophet.
Open our eyes, ears, and hearts
that we may appreciate salvation
and listen to the voice
   of the Prophet, Jesus Christ,
as well as those prophets
   whom you send in our time
to shake us up
   so that we may turn to Jesus and to you
with all our hearts.

We honor you, Mary, as the Queen
   of the prophets.
Pray for us
that we may always be open
   to the grace of the Holy Spirit
and to the voice of those who call us
   to total conversion. Amen.

## 20
## Mary and the Magi

"Jesus was born at Bethlehem in Judea during the reign of Herod. After his birth, astrologers from the east arrived in Jerusalem asking, 'Where is the child who is born to be king of the Jews? We observed the rising of his star and we have come to pay him homage.' King Herod was greatly perturbed when he heard this; and so was the whole of Jerusalem. He called a meeting of the chief priests and lawyers of the Jewish people and put before them the question: 'Where is it that the Messiah is to be born?' 'At Bethlehem in Judea,' they replied; and they referred him to the prophecy which reads: 'Bethlehem in the land of Judah, you are by no means least in the eyes of the rulers of Judah; for out of you shall come a leader to be the shepherd of my people Israel.'

"Herod next called the astrologers to meet him in private, and ascertained from them the time when the star had appeared. He then sent them on to Bethlehem and said, 'Go and make a careful inquiry for the child. When you have found him, report to me so that I may go myself and pay him homage.'

"They set out at the king's bidding; and the star which they had seen at its rising went ahead of them until it stopped above the place where the child lay. At the sight of the star, they were overjoyed. Entering the house, they saw the child with Mary, his mother, and did him homage. Then they opened their treasures and offered him gifts, gold, frankincense and myrrh. On being warned in a dream not to go back to Herod, they returned home another way" (Mt 2:1-12).

This narrative is much more than the account of an event. It is a profound vision about Jesus, the light of all nations, the center and summit of all history. The truly religious men of all ages rejoice in his coming. And, if the joy of these men who represent the godly people is so great, how great then must be Mary's joy when realizing the first fulfillment of the prophecy of Simeon: that her Son is to be the light of all nations. Again we see the relatedness of Mary to the evangelization of all the world. We cannot truly venerate her without an ardent zeal for the salvation of all people to know and praise his name.

"They saw the child with Mary his mother." The proclamation of all that God has done for Mary and the correct veneration of her can do much to prepare the way for faith in Jesus. Not long ago, a concrete experience strengthened this conviction in me. In Singapore — a city in Asia having a small minority of Christians — every Saturday 20,000 persons come to a novena honoring Our Lady of Perpetual Help where the basic truths of our faith are preached in order that all may find Jesus with Mary his Mother. The majority of participants are non-Christian; and each year many hundreds enter the life of the Church while others continue to pray to Mary and to meditate constantly upon the Gospel of Christ.

The event which we celebrate at Epiphany according to the narrative of Matthew proclaims a joyful fulfillment of the prophecy of Isaiah: "You shall see and be radiant, your heart shall thrill and rejoice, because the abundance of the sea shall be turned to you, the wealth of the nations shall come to you. A multitude of camels shall cover you. . . . All those from Sheba shall come. They shall bring gold and frankincense, and shall proclaim the praise of the Lord'' (Is 60:5-6).

The coming of Christ reaches out to all ages and to all people of good will. Mary rejoices in all who give themselves to Jesus in the purity of their heart symbolized by the gold. The purity of motives with which so many seek and find the Lord is related to the immaculate heart of Mary who serves God with the purity of her entire being. Her heart overflows with joy when she sees the multitudes who seek and find her Son, Jesus, because of the purity of their motives.

The Wise Men offer frankincense, the symbol of adoration. Mary leads the choir of all who praise the Lord and adore him in all their lives. If we come to Mary, we can learn from her how to *follow Christ as true adorers of the Father*. When Jesus, later in his ministry, speaks to the woman of Samaria on the great mystery that God wants adorers ''in spirit and truth,'' he surely remembers the example of his own Mother.

The Wise Men who seek and find the Lord offer myrrh which reminds us of the death and sepulcher of Christ. When later on, Mary of Bethany, the sister of Lazarus, anoints the feet of Jesus with a pound of a very costly perfume, Jesus spells out the meaning of what she does: ''Let her keep it until the day when she prepares for my burial'' (Jn 12:7). Mary, the Mother of Jesus, is closest to Jesus beneath the Cross and at the sepulcher where he was buried. Her presence is the final test of her adoration of God in truth and fullness which comes from the Holy Spirit.

We praise you, Father almighty,
for having sent your Christ to all nations.
Make us grateful for the gift of faith
that we may all become a living Gospel
    for those whom we meet.
Send workers into your vineyard.
Awaken in your Church a new zeal
    to bring the Good News to all,
that all might rejoice in Christ
and unite themselves with him
who, in his humanity,
    is the perfect adorer of your name.
Cleanse our hearts, our intentions,
that we may be able to offer you
    all that we think, desire and do
as a pure sacrifice united with Christ.
May your Holy Spirit teach us
    how to praise your name
and how to understand the meaning
    of frustration and suffering
so that we may unite them
    with the one Eucharist offered by Christ.

O Mary, you have offered yourself to God
    as pure gold.
Seeing your joy at the Epiphany,
    we ask you to pray for us
that we might consider it
    the greatest privilege
to be sent as messengers of the Good News
and to preach the Gospel,
    whatever may be the cost. Amen.

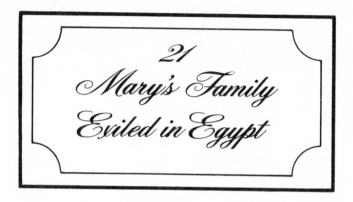

21
Mary's Family
Exiled in Egypt

"An angel of the Lord appeared to Joseph in a dream and said to him, 'Rise up and take the child and his mother and escape with them to Egypt and stay there until I tell you, for Herod is going to search for the child to do away with him.' So Joseph rose from sleep and, taking mother and child by night, he went away with them to Egypt and there he stayed until Herod's death. This was to fulfill what the Lord had declared to the prophet: 'I called my son out of Egypt.'

"When Herod saw how the astrologers had tricked him, he fell into a passion and gave orders for the massacre of all boys two years old or less in Bethlehem and its neighborhood. This corresponded with the time he had ascertained from the astrologers. So the words spoken through Jeremiah, the prophet, were fulfilled: 'A voice was heard in Ramah, wailing and loud laments; it was Rachel weeping for her children and refusing all consolation because they were no more' '' (Mt 2:13-18).

When Mary and Joseph have to escape into Egypt to save the life of the Child in the land of exile, the prophecy of Simeon comes true. The innocent One, the holy One becomes a sign of contradiction. While people come from far to seek him, to rejoice in his presence and offer themselves to his service, Herod, the king of Judah, tries to kill him and becomes, indeed, the murderer of many children.

A special divine providence protects the Child and his Mother, and Joseph is chosen to be the visible sign of this protection.

The Holy Family relives the history of salvation which is a history of exodus and liberation. Joseph, the patriarch, was sold by his brothers and brought as a slave to Egypt to become savior to his brothers. The patriarch Jacob had to go to Egypt, and Moses and the people suffered there under fierce oppression until the Lord freed them from the land of slavery.

Through the prophet Hosea, God calls his people, "my sons"; for in the liberation of Israel, God acts as Father. "When Israel was a child I loved him, out of Egypt I called my son" (Hos 11:1). All this comes to full truth in Jesus who with Joseph and his Mother has to escape to Egypt and experience this saving action of the Father. He is the beloved Son and yet he suffers with the downtrodden, with the homeless, and the persecuted.

During our lifetime, we have seen millions of people in various parts of the world who were driven out of their fatherland. Millions of others are migrants looking for work and a piece of bread. No book can contain all the misery and humiliation endured by them. May they remember the experience of Joseph and Mary and Jesus in Egypt. May they turn to Mary in their need, and experience the love of the heavenly Father. If Jesus has taken upon himself this painful exodus, others should not consider this as meaningless. And yet we honor the Holy Family who escaped into Egypt only if we sympathize with the homeless, with the millions of people who live in camps or have to hide their identities because no one wants them.

Holy Scripture does not tell us that Mary came to know about the massacre in Bethlehem, but the thought of it was with Mary and Joseph for the time they spent in Egypt. When they returned to the land of Galilee, they heard about this and about other crimes of Herod; how great must have been her *compassion and the suffering of her immaculate heart.* Indeed the prophecy of Simeon stayed with her always.

**All-holy God, your ways are wonderful,**
**your wisdom**
    **is above all our human thoughts.**
**We thank you that through the suffering**
    **of Jesus, of Mary and Joseph**
**in the land of exile,**
**you have brought redemption**
    **for the terrible suffering**
**of those who are persecuted, downtrodden,**
    **and homeless.**
**We pray for them,**
**that they may not suffer in vain**
    **and that their cry may be heard.**

O Mary, we pray to you,
  the Mother of Perpetual Help.
May all believers learn
  from your generosity;
may the rulers of the countries honor God,
  the one Father,
by a greater concern for those who are
  rejected, lonely, and homeless.
Pray for us that we may learn compassion,
and unite our actions in favor of those
  who are most in need. Amen.

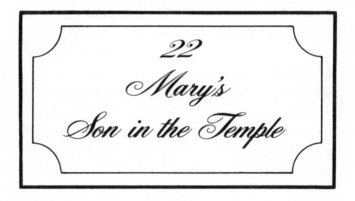

*22*
*Mary's*
*Son in the Temple*

"They returned to Galilee to their own town of Nazareth. The child grew big and strong and full of wisdom; and God's favor was upon him" (Lk 2:39-40).

God guided Joseph and Mary to bring the child from the land of exile to Galilee, the most humble part of Israel. There, in the house of prayer in Nazareth, Jesus grows up. The evangelist underlines the true humanity of Jesus. Like other children, Jesus grows up; but unlike others, he is already full of wisdom and radiant in the grace of God. Mary helps Jesus to walk, to talk, to relate to people with affection;

she stimulates his growth in self-awareness and personal freedom. In this period of growth, Mary, doubtless, plays a privileged role. Like a spotless mirror, she reflects the divine love; she is, with Joseph, the one who sings the song of the Servant, and her life is the best commentary of it. As Jesus grows each day, she can better understand this wonderful prophecy. Hers is the privilege to see the graciousness of Jesus, the spontaneity of his prayer life, his kindness in helping others.

"Now it was the practice of his parents to go to Jerusalem every year for the Passover festival; and when Jesus was 12, they made the pilgrimage as usual. When the festive season was over and they started for home, the boy Jesus stayed behind in Jerusalem. His parents did not know of this; but thinking that he was with the party, they journeyed on for a whole day and only then did they begin looking for him among their friends and relatives. As they could not find him, they returned to Jerusalem to look for him; and after three days, they found him sitting in the Temple, surrounded by the teachers, listening to them and asking them questions. All who heard him were amazed at his intelligence and his answers.

"His parents were astonished to see him there and his mother said to him, 'My Son, why have you treated us like this? Your father and I have been searching for you in great anxiety.' 'What made you search?' he said. 'Did you not know that I was bound to be in my Father's house?' But they did not understand what he meant. Then he went back with them to Nazareth, and continued to be under their mother treasured up all these things in her heart. As Jesus grew up, he advanced in wisdom and in favor with God and men" (Lk 2:41-52).

The episode in the Temple is a great prophecy: Christ detaching himself from his family to begin his pilgrimage. It entails shock and great anxiety. Up to that point, Jesus had shown a gracious dependence on Mary and Joseph. He evidently had never undertaken anything without the knowledge of his parents. And now, suddenly, he reveals to Mary his mission which involves suffering and the profound experience of the exodus. The event foreshadows the time when Jesus will leave his home in Nazareth to spend 40 days in the desert and later to become a pilgrim as the living Gospel in Galilee and Judea. The prophecy goes even beyond that detachment: the three days filled with anguish give a glimpse of the future — the three days between the death of Jesus on the Cross and his Resurrection.

This Biblical text is of paramount importance. It is the first time we hear Jesus call the almighty God "Father." He does not just say, "Father," he says, "My Father." It is that profound expression of the relationship between Jesus and the One who sent him. It is the word that engraves itself more than any other word in the memory of the Church throughout the centuries. This word of Jesus spoken in the Temple after his surprising separation from Mary and Joseph indicates the new family, the whole family of the redeemed that is based upon the unique relationship of Jesus of Nazareth to the Fatherhood of God.

This word, "Abba, Father," is to be the last word that Jesus speaks on the Cross. Each Israelite ends his day with a prayer to Yahweh: "Into thy hands, I entrust my spirit." On the Cross, however, Jesus adds the one word "Father" to the traditional prayer. He has manifested him as the Father of all. Totally new horizons open up in the history of salvation, and the risen Lord speaking to Mary Magdalene makes clear the dimensions of the new family, "my Father and your Father." Before his ascension, he will promise the Holy Spirit, referring again to that unique name of Father: "And mark this, I am sending upon you my Father's promised gift, so stay here in this city until you are armed with power from above" (Lk 24:49).

The coming of the Holy Spirit upon the apostles gathered around Mary will give life to the new family promised by the prophetic event in the Temple when 12-year-old Jesus reveals his relationship to the Almighty for the first time. The new family of God will manifest itself everywhere throughout history where people are moved by the Spirit of God and recognize themselves as sons and daughters of God. "You did not receive a spirit of slavery . . . but a spirit of adoption enabling you to cry, 'Abba, Father!' The Spirit himself gives witness with our spirit that we are children of God" (Rom 8:15-16).

Mary, the Mother of Jesus of Nazareth, is called to enter into a new depth of awareness. Her role is even greater: she is to be the mother of the Church; hers is a motherhood in the new family of God based on the relationship of Jesus to his heavenly Father and the Holy Spirit. Mary, strong in faith and filled with motherly love, lives in the nearness of Jesus; but she is also to undergo the dark night of faith. In spite of her absolute purity and docility, she is not able at once to understand the full depth of the events nor the words of Jesus. However, all that she is, does, and says is a prayer that Jesus may reveal to her the mystery and the words he speaks in this event. She treasures up his words in her heart until she comes to a full understanding.

In the lives of Jesus and Mary, there is no place for what we call "conversion." In them, there is no shadow of sin but *they too live under the law of growth*. It is remarkable that Luke, in one and the same chapter, twice emphasizes that Jesus advanced in wisdom and in favor with God and man. This is important too for the Church in her gradual grasping of her mission and in the ongoing effort of interpreting the signs of the times.

**We thank you,**
  **Father of our Lord**
  **Jesus Christ**
**and our Father,**
**that in the Temple you have manifested**
  **the wisdom of your Son, Jesus.**
**We shall never be able to thank you enough**
**for the gladdening news**
  **that there is, among us, a Brother**
**who can call you with full right**
  **"my Father,"**
**and who entitles us to join him**

in the new family
and to call you "our Father."
Lord God, our Father,
make us holy, make us one in your love.

We thank you, O Mary,
for your motherly care of Jesus
   our brother and our Lord.
We are deeply touched
   by the pain and anguish of your heart
in that prophetic event foreshadowing
   three even more anguishing days
after the death of your Son, Jesus Christ.
Pray for us
that we may treasure up the words
   of Jesus in our hearts as you did
and that we may be patient and faithful
   in our common effort
to reach a deeper understanding
   of the words of Jesus
and a fuller discernment of the signs
   of the times. Amen.

## 23
## Mary at Cana

"There was a wedding at Cana in Galilee.
The mother of Jesus was there, and Jesus and

his disciples were guests also. The wine gave out, so Jesus' mother said to him, 'They have no wine left.' He answered, 'O woman, what does this mean for you and me? My hour has not yet come.' His mother said to the servants, 'Do whatever he tells you.' There were six stone water jars standing near, of the kind used for Jewish rites of purification; each held from twenty to thirty gallons. Jesus said to the servants, 'Fill the jars with water.' And they filled them to the brim. 'Now draw some off,' he ordered, 'and take it to the steward of the feast'; and they did so. The steward tasted the water now turned into wine, not knowing its source, though the servants who had drawn the water knew. He hailed the bridegroom and said, 'Everyone serves the best wine first and waits until the guests have drunk freely before serving the poorer sort; but you have kept the best wine till now.' This deed at Cana in Galilee is the first of the signs by which Jesus revealed his glory and led his disciples to believe in him'' (Jn 2:1-11).

This narrative brings the image of Mary down to earth and exalts her unto heaven. It is at the same time a manifestation of Mary's loving attention to the earthly needs of people and her prophetic intuition of an event that goes far beyond daily life. As in the house of Zechariah, so again we find her in Cana as a humble servant who helps out in the household. It is probably a gesture of courtesy toward Mary that Jesus and his disciples are invited. The fact that he comes with quite a number of friends might partially be the cause of the embarrassment — that the wine ran out.

That she brings the matter before her Son expresses her goodness and indicates inspiration by the Holy Spirit. She does not tell Jesus what to do. Her prayer is courageous and at the same time humble.

This is a model for our prayer. Are we not sometimes tempted to tell God what he should do instead of simply opening our needs to him and asking him for the grace that our wills may be totally conformed to his will? In a humble prayer like that of Mary, we begin to discover dimensions far beyond our immediate needs, and we come to realize that the Lord always knows better what is truly good for us.

Jesus' miracle at Cana as a response to his Mother is a prophetic event. Each word and action is rich in meaning and opens up new horizons. The word of Mary to the servants, a word that seems directed to each of us, deserves our special attention: "Do whatever he tells you." This is at the heart of true Marian devotion. Mary our mother has no greater desire than to draw all our attention, love, and obedience to Jesus. We honor her as we follow him and do whatever he tells us by his word, grace, life and death as well as all the events of his life.

The prayer of Mary occasions the first great sign of Jesus in which he reveals his divine power. She is like a friend of an artist who sometimes through a humble suggestion gives the artist a fuller insight into his work. The first response of Jesus to Mary in this scene is translated in various ways, but the way he addresses her must be seen in its context. It contains no refusal or blame.

Jesus does not say, "Mother," but rather, "Woman." It is the same expression used in one of the opening scenes of the Bible, where God promises: "I will put enmity between you and the woman" (Gn 3:15). On the Cross Jesus again addresses his Mother as "Woman"; and the vision of the great woman found in the book of Genesis comes to its full magnitude in the book of Revelation, chapter 12. In the eyes of Jesus, in that solemn moment at Cana, Mary is more than his "private" mother. She is the great sign of promise, a prophetic sign affirmed by the first miracle which Jesus works in view of her, the "Woman."

Jesus says, "My hour has not yet come." The present event, notable as it is, has to be read in the light of the exalted hour of Jesus when he is to shed the blood of the new and eternal covenant in a wedding of himself forever with redeemed humanity. Christ is the spouse who preserves the best wine until the end.

The embarrassment of the spouses at Cana, which gives rise to such a great miracle, is a modest symbol of the profound suffering in which the wedding between Christ and the Church is rehearsed. Mary is present to both events. She will always invite and urge us: "Do whatever he tells you." And her word is both an exhortation and a gift.

We praise you,
　Father of our Lord Jesus Christ;
for in this event

you have revealed the new Adam
and the new Eve, the immaculate woman,
the model of the Church.
We thank you, for by your Spirit
   you have inspired the humble prayer
which gives rise to the first sign
   of our salvation.
Grant to us your grace
that in this event
   and in all events of our lives
we may discover the profound meaning
   of salvation.

O Mary, how beautiful
   is your trusting prayer!
You know how to honor Jesus
   by your prayer.
Pray for us that we, like you at Cana,
may learn to intercede for each other,
being always ready
   to bear each other's burdens. Amen.

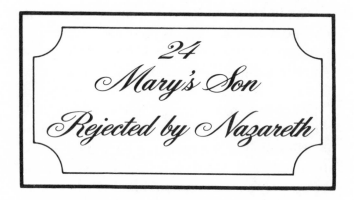

24
Mary's Son
Rejected by Nazareth

"Hear, O heavens, and give ear, O earth, for
the Lord has spoken: Sons have I reared and
brought up, but they have rebelled against me.

The ox knows its owner, and the ass, its master's grip; but Israel does not know. My people do not understand" (Is 1:2-3).

The heart of the prophet Isaiah must have been pierced when the Lord bade him to announce this terrible suffering of God's own heart. How must have been pierced, then, the heart of Mary when she experienced the fulfillment of this prophecy in her hometown of Nazareth. The Gospel of Saint Luke gives us a lively description.

"Then Jesus, armed with the power of the Spirit, returned to Galilee; and reports about him spread through the whole countryside. He taught in their synagogues and all men sang his praises.

"So he came to Nazareth, where he had been brought up, and went to the synagogue on the Sabbath day as he regularly did. He stood up to read the lesson and was handed the scroll of the prophet Isaiah. He opened the scroll and found the passage which says:

'The Spirit of the Lord is upon me because he has anointed me. He has sent me:
to announce good news to the poor,
to proclaim release for prisoners and recovery of sight for the blind,
to let broken victims go free,
to proclaim the year of the Lord's favor.'

"He rolled up the scroll, gave it back to the attendant, and sat down; and all eyes in the synagogue were fixed on him. He began to speak: 'Today,' he said, 'in your hearing, this text has come true.' There was a general stir of admiration; they were surprised that words of such grace should fall from his lips. 'Is not this

Joseph's son?' they asked. Then Jesus said, 'No doubt you will quote the proverb to me, "Physician heal yourself," and say, "We have heard of all your doings at Capernaum; do the same here in your own hometown." I tell you this,' he went on, 'no prophet is recognized in his own country. There were many widows in Israel, you may be sure, in Elijah's time, when for three years and six months the skies never opened, and famine lay hard over the whole country; yet it was to none of these that Elijah was sent, but to a widow at Sarepta in the territory of Sidon. Again, in the time of the prophet Elisha there were many lepers in Israel, and not one of them was healed, but only Naaman the Syrian.'

"At these words, the whole congregation was infuriated. They rose up and threw him out of the town, leading him to the brow of the hill on which it was built, and meaning to hurl him over the edge. But he walked straight through them all and went away" (Lk 4:14-30).

This passage of great relevance is similar in story to Matthew 13:53-58 and Mark 6:1-6 where the people refer explicitly to Mary, "Is not this the carpenter, the son of Mary?" The Mother of Jesus was most probably present at these happenings. Jesus was deeply hurt: "He was taken aback by their want of faith" (Mk 6:6). How great must have been the hurt in Mary's heart!

We cannot avoid asking the question, "Why was Jesus rejected by his own townsfolk?" The response seems to be: Jesus came from humble people. Everyone knew his Mother, Mary, and that the family lived in lowly social conditions.

Under these circumstances, Jesus presents himself explicitly as the Servant of God and man. Thus, Jesus, by his very origin, by his life style and by his word, thoroughly rejects the false Messianic expectations. So many had anticipated a national hero, and the Gospel text indicates that his own wanted him to be a miracle worker for their own greater glory. They were jealous because he had made his home in Capernaum and had worked great signs in that place. Thus, the townspeople felt that he was sinning against their collective interests.

This conduct of the people of Nazareth symbolically expresses the sin of a great part of Israel. The high priest, the Pharisees, the powerful, look on religion as a means; and had Jesus allowed himself to be used for their self-interests, he would have served their false purposes and would have violated his true mission as Servant of Yahweh. Because he refused to play into the hands of such people, Jesus was rejected and scorned. No one other than Mary, the humble handmaid of God, could so profoundly have understood this conflict between the Servant of God and the false Messianic expectation. This sad event in Nazareth was, for Mary, a prophecy of what would happen on Calvary.

We see Mary, the Mother of Jesus and our mother, as one who suffered in this moment and throughout the coming years for all the sins of humankind, for all the collective egotism, arrogance, and pride which lead to the rejection of Christ the Servant. All this serves as motive to venerate Mary who teaches us *how to follow Jesus in humility and detachment,* sharing in

Christ's suffering. Honoring Mary means
never using the Church for personal gain, pres-
tige, wealth, or power. Rather, it means honoring the Church as humble servants of Christ.

Almighty and all-merciful God,
   teach us all to know the name
   of Jesus,
   "Servant of God."
Protect your Church
   that, with Mary the humble handmaid,
she may always be a sign
   of Christ the Savior.
Open the eyes of those
   who wrongly seek honor and favors
instead of following Christ,
crucified for us.


O Mary, we honor your suffering,
your pain caused by those whom you loved.
How deep must have been the wound
   in your heart
when you saw Jesus rejected
   by your neighbors!
We are all written into your heart
and we should know how deeply we wound
   your heart
when we refuse to accept Christ
   as the Servant
and follow him in humility as you did.
Pray for us
that we may come to accept
   all the frustrations and sufferings
with which the Lord allows us

to be afflicted on this road of salvation,
and thus come to know more intensely
Christ, the suffering Servant,
and you, his Mother,
   who followed him on his road. Amen.

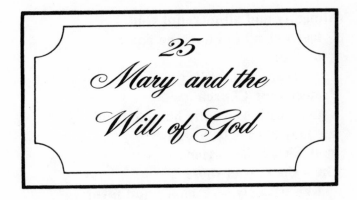

*25*
*Mary and the Will of God*

"Jesus entered a house; and once more such a crowd collected round them that they had no chance to eat. When his family heard of this, they set out to take charge of him. 'He is out of his mind,' they said. Also the doctors of the Law who had come from Jerusalem said, 'He is possessed by Beelzebub,' and 'He drives out devils by the prince of devils.' He called them to come forward and spoke to them in parables. 'How can Satan drive out Satan? If a kingdom is divided against itself, that kingdom cannot stand; and if Satan is in rebellion against himself, he is divided and cannot stand; and that is the end of him. On the other hand, no one can break into a strong man's house and make off with his goods unless he has first tied the strong man up; then he can ransack the house. I tell you this: No sin, no slander of man is beyond forgiveness, but whoever slanders the Holy

Spirit can never be forgiven; he is guilty of eternal sin.' He said this because they had declared that he was possessed by an unclean spirit.

"Then his mother and his brothers arrived and, remaining outside, sent in a message asking him to come out to them. A crowd was sitting round as word was brought to him: 'Your mother and your brothers are outside asking for you.' He replied, 'Who is my mother? Who are my brothers?' And looking around at those who were sitting in the circle about him, he said, 'Here are my mother and my brothers. Whoever does the will of God is my brother, my sister, my mother' " (Mk 3:20-35).

This narrative may be surprising to those who have a tender devotion to Mary, but it would be erroneous to think that Mary, the Mother of Jesus, was among those who said, "He is out of his mind." She surely was not a possessive mother. She allowed her Son to manage his own affairs. In fact, Mary's suffering must have been great, seeing the lack of faith and reverence toward her Son by the members of her own family! It seems that she was most painfully caught up in their maneuver. Most likely, she was present in order to bridle their tongues and to bring them to a proper frame of mind.

These words of Jesus indicate a detachment from his natural family, and even from his Mother as far as physical motherhood is concerned. They are an expression of the same detachment or exodus which we have seen in the narrative about Jesus in the Temple. "What made you search? Did you not know that I was bound to be in my Father's house?" Now it became even clearer that Jesus had not come to build up his own little family, but rather to bring into being a world-wide family of disciples, a family based entirely upon the universal fatherhood of almighty God, his Father, and himself as brother of all.

In this perspective, then, we can understand our own family, particularly when the family tries to obstruct our total adherence to the kingdom of God. Let us never forget, too, that detachment is only one aspect. It is part of the wonderful expression of the Good News: Those who follow Christ wholeheartedly, whatever may be the price, are as dear to him as brothers and sisters are. Moreover, they are as dear to him as his Mother. This expression of our Master's love for us also helps us to better understand a similar and even more profound expression: "As the Father has loved me, so I have loved you" (Jn 15:9).

Mary, totally consecrated to the kingdom of the Father and to the mission of the Servant of God, is never an obstacle to the mission of Christ. On the contrary, her entire life helps us to understand the meaning of detachment, of exodus as she follows Christ in his most crucial moments, particularly in this humiliating circumstance, and more so when she stands beneath the Cross. If we are ready to follow Mary along this road, then perhaps in moments of deepest suffering we will more fully understand *what it means to be as dear to Jesus as his Mother;* we will hear and understand the words: "Son, behold your mother!"

Thus we come to realize that this response of Jesus to those who did not yet know that he was the cornerstone of a new universal family does not at all estrange us from Mary; rather, it helps us to understand her role in the new family of God. And we know that she will be present to us in moments of severest temptation if only we are ready to follow the Servant of God.

We praise you, Father of our Lord Jesus,
that in your beloved Son
   you have given us the privilege
of belonging to your family
and of calling you, with Jesus, Father.
We thank you, Jesus,
   for your infinite love that is as tender
   as the love of a mother
and even more tender
   than that of the greatest mother,
   your own.
If we join you in love for your Mother
and come to realize more completely
   how tenderly you loved her,
we can come closer to you
   and understand more deeply
how much you love us when, like Mary,
   we listen to your Word,
treasure it up in our heart,
ready to put it into practice.
   Grant us, O Lord,
the ability to be true listeners
   of your Word,
able to respond with all our hearts
   in all our lives.

O Mary, in the midst of the pain
caused by members of your family,
you rejoiced,
assured by your Son
   that he loves all of us, your children,
with the same love with which he loves you.
Knowing this, we also know
   how great your love is for us
when we put all our trust in Jesus.
Pray for us, O Mary, that we may be
   grateful for this privilege
and that nothing in this world
   will hinder us from following Christ
wholeheartedly
as members of the new family which honors
   the one Father in heaven
and pays tribute also to you,
   the mother of the living. Amen.

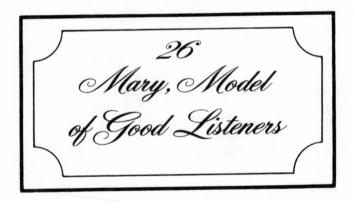

# 26
# Mary, Model of Good Listeners

"While he was speaking thus, a woman in the crowd called out, 'Happy the womb that carried you and the breasts that suckled you!' He rejoined, 'Rather, happy are those who hear the word of God and keep it' " (Lk 11:27-28).

Jesus had driven out a devil and had healed the man with a speech defect so that he could speak properly and praise the Lord. Those in high positions in the synagogue have just scorned Jesus, whereas the contrasting figure is the humble woman in the crowd who, with great admiration and faith, praises Jesus by praising his Mother. Jesus accepts this beautiful expression of human sentiment but, as always, gives it a deeper meaning. Not wanting to diminish the glory of his Mother, he emphasizes the one dimension that is the true glory of Mary; she is the mother in the new family of God whose openness to the Word of God is dedicated to living the truth.

This is consistent with the words of St. Luke in his Gospel. He repeatedly shows Mary as the model of faith. From the moment of the incarnation: "Behold, here am I, the servant of the Lord." At the event of the Visitation: "Happy is she who has had faith that the Lord's promise would be fulfilled." In her silent and yet eloquent response to the song of the angels and the message of the shepherds: "Mary treasured up all these events and pondered over them." And again, at the event in the Temple when Jesus shows his detachment from his natural family: "His mother treasured up all these things in her heart."

In the discourse on the Mount, Jesus most solemnly teaches this distinctive characteristic of his new family: It is not sufficient to call oneself his disciple; what is needed is openness to his Word as a listener and a responder. "Not everyone who calls me 'Lord, Lord' will enter the kingdom of heaven, but only those who do the will of my heavenly Father. . . . The one who hears these words of mine and acts on them is like a man who had the sense to build his house on rock'' (Mt 7:21-24).

Thus, Jesus reveals to us the true motherhood of Mary as the model of the Church: She lives by every word that comes from the mouth of God and is totally dedicated to act upon that word.

The future of Christianity depends greatly upon each community knowing how to celebrate the Eucharist, the memorial of our Lord's suffering, death and Resurrection, which means also being prepared to live according to this mystery. We can be sure of her intercession if we are willing to learn from her and to follow her example. She is the perfect Eucharistic person — that is, the person who remembers with perfect gratitude, and who inspires fidelity in our commitment to the kingdom of God.

If we want to be authentic members of the new family grounded on faith in Christ, then we have to learn more deeply the art of discovering the signs of God's presence. We must listen to his Word: in all of creation; in the human person, as image and likeness of God; in the saints and the prophets; and in the wonderful message of the sacraments — always relying on the grace of the Holy Spirit to help us discover the message and the will of God. With Mary the Virgin, *we shall daily meditate upon the Holy Scriptures;* we shall also give full attention to the *magisterium* (teaching authority) of the Church in order to better understand the total message of Christ. However, the heart of the matter is always what Mary teaches us, "Do whatever he tells you."

Glory and praise to you, all-holy God,
for through all your works
    you speak to us.
Everything directs our attention
    to your only begotten Son
who is your final Word to us,
the full revelation
    of your love and your will.
Send us your Holy Spirit
    that we may always listen to your Word
with a pure heart
and with a firm purpose to act accordingly.

O Mary, pray for us
that the Lord may give us,
    as he gave to you,
a memory filled with gratitude,
so that each day we may learn
    how to celebrate the Eucharist properly,
and to live our life in grateful response
to all of God's gifts. Amen.

## 27
## Mary,
## Mother of Sorrows

"Near the cross where Jesus hung there stood his mother (Jn 19:25).

We have accompanied Mary on the various stations of her exodus, of her detachment, and of her pilgrimage. We have seen her when, with Child, she had to leave home and give birth to Jesus as the poorest of all pilgrims. When the prophet Simeon announces to Mary that a sword would pierce her heart, she is already acquainted with that thought. Crossing the desert with Joseph and the Child to live as migrants in Egypt — thus recalling the history of her people — Mary anticipates the final rejection of Jesus through his own people. The three days of anguish in seeking and finally finding Jesus in the Temple foretell future anxiety. No one suffers as deeply as his Mother when Jesus does not find faith among those whom God has especially prepared by his revelation.

Mary is not present at the triumphant entry of Jesus into Jerusalem, but she is present — under the Cross — at the decisive hour of the redemption of the world. More than a mother suffers at childbirth, Mary suffers on hearing the words of anguish from Jesus, "My God, my God, why hast thou forsaken me?" No less shaken in heart than Jesus is, she is also one with him when he entrusts himself totally into the hands of his Father. During the Passion and death of Jesus, Mary lives the pain and the beatitude that no one can know as well as Jesus himself: "Blessed are the sorrowful, for they will be consoled." With Jesus, she suffers on behalf of our sins — she who is immaculate, never touched by any sin. She suffers in redemptive compassion. Her sorrow expresses faith and love. It is a sign of her role in the new family in which everyone knows the law of Christ, that is, to bear each other's burdens. *United with Christ, Mary bears our burdens.*

Mary knows the name of Jesus, "the Covenant of the people"; she lives the mystery of saving solidarity (saving mutual dependence) of which the apostle of the gentiles will speak so convincingly: "It is now my happiness to suffer for you. This is my way of helping to complete, in my poor flesh, the complete record of Christ's affliction still to be endured, for the sake of his body which is the Church" (Col 1:24). Mary, the deaconess (servant) of salvation has lived this mystery in an outstanding way as the new Eve totally associated with the new Adam. It is not that Jesus' suffering would not be complete without Mary's sufferings. On the contrary, it is the overflowing power of Christ's death and Resurrection that gives, first to Mary and then to all the disciples of Christ, the power to share in his saving solidarity.

When we call Mary the new Eve, "co-redemptrix," or deaconess of salvation, this in no way denies that Christ alone is our Mediator, our Savior, our Redeemer; rather, it accentuates the superabundance of Christ's suffering, death and Resurrection, and offers praise and thanksgiving to our Mediator and Redeemer who allows us to be humble sharers in the work of redemption. Therefore we can, with Paul, offer thanksgiving even for our frustrations and sufferings; it is not thanksgiving for suffering as such, but for the transfiguration of suffering and death in the saving solidarity with the death and Resurrection of Christ. Our share cannot be understood without fully acknowledging the privileged share of the new Eve, Mary.

A personal experience helped me and may help others to understand this great mystery of sharing in Christ's redemptive sufferings. More than 20 years ago, I paid a visit to a famous Protestant theologian who once had been a Catholic priest and teacher of dogmatic theology. Because of the celibacy issue, he had left not only the priesthood but also his Church. He had been ill for some time when I went to see him. With a gesture of welcome, he said, "After 40 years, you are the first priest to visit me." We had a long and very good talk; it became clear to me that, in his heart, he still belonged to the Catholic Church. But, how could I hope that he would have the courage to take the step he somehow desired, having been a famous man in his Church?

I wrote to a former companion of his, Joseph Bernhardt, who in the era of modernism and antimodernism had had difficulty with the Church. He got married, later returned to the Church, and in Hitler's time had been one of the most courageous witnesses to the faith. I asked him whether he would visit his former friend and listen to the desires of his heart. He did and he wrote to me: "Like you, I think his conscience does not yet seem to be settled; only the prayer and sacrifice of a saint can obtain such a great grace."

I spoke about this matter to one of my penitents whom I considered a saint. I knew that she would join us in our prayers. But she did more; spontaneously, she offered her life, if such an offer could bring the grace to that man whom I had told her had always remained faithful in his devotion to Mary. She fell into a deadly illness, suffering great pain, but refused any medication. Before her death, she expressed her firm trust that the Lord had heard our prayers. She died on the feast of the Epiphany. Meanwhile, the man for whom we had been praying had been hospitalized. Without warning, he asked his attending physician: "What would the world say if, after all, I would return to the Catholic Church?" The inspired response was another question: "Dear Professor! In a few weeks you will have only one question: 'What did God say?' " Quickly, he urged the physician to call the priest immediately. He made his confession and called his wife to declare his intention to die as a member of the Catholic Church.

Whatever may be our active share in the mystery of redemption, it is always the result of the Passion, death, and Resurrection of our

Lord Jesus Christ. And we shall never forget
the special share which Mary has had and continues to have in this great mystery.

We praise you,
   all-holy and all-merciful Father,
for the Passion, death, and Resurrection
   of Jesus, your Son,
that transformed the meaning
   of our suffering and our death.
We are redeemed from the slavery of sin
if we gratefully and actively
   enter into the mystery of redemption.
We praise you for the mission you have
   entrusted to Mary, the new Eve,
the sorrowful Mother in this mystery.
Make us grateful and give us the courage
   to take upon ourselves our cross
and to bear a part of the burden
   of our brothers and sisters.


O sorrowful Mother of Jesus,
you are blessed,
for your suffering was not like that
   of those who are caught
   in the web of social evil
   and the emptiness of a selfish world.
Yours was a suffering
   similar to that of Christ.
You who have suffered with faith,
   with hope, and with love for all of us,
pray for us that we may, with you,
follow Christ on the way of the Cross.
   Thank you. Amen.

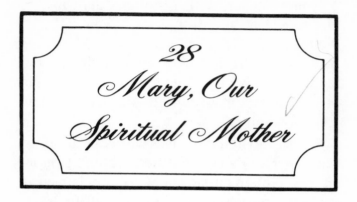

*28*
*Mary, Our*
*Spiritual Mother*

"Jesus saw his mother with the disciple he loved standing beside her. He said to her, 'Woman, there is your son'; and to the disciple, 'There is your mother'; and from that moment, the disciple took her into his home" (Jn 19:26-27).

Aware that his death was approaching, Jesus, as the head of a small family, takes care of his Mother by entrusting her to his best and most faithful friend, the virginal disciple, John. What every thoughtful man does on his deathbed, Christ does on the altar of the Cross, and he does it with unique tenderness. His word and his gesture have, however, a much broader sense; this is even indicated by the careful wording of the text. The Gospel of John says that Jesus saw "his mother." Then when Jesus addresses her, he calls her "woman." He addresses her not only as his Mother but as the "woman" spoken of in Chapter 3 of Genesis. We have seen this prophetic meaning in the word "woman" when Mary played a providential role in the first miracle of Jesus at the beginning of his public life. On Calvary he not only entrusts his Mother to John but he invites him to see in his Mother the "woman" predicted in the book of Genesis. Thus Jesus makes clear that he now speaks on the level of the new family of which he, the new Adam, is the head, and in which his Mother, the new Eve, has a unique role.

We are invited by these words of Jesus to venerate Mary's spiritual motherhood. Honoring this role and mission of Mary, proclaimed at the moment of the great exodus when Jesus gave his life for us on the Cross, we can never forget the detachment entailed as well as the subsequent life of the exodus. Thus, when we are invited with John to look at Mary as our mother, *we stand with profound veneration before the new Eve,* the mother of the living, the great sign of which the Book of Revelation speaks.

We love our mother with the love of Jesus, and we love her gratefully because she has brought us to life in the pangs of childbirth suffered by Christ himself on the Cross and suffered by her also.

The spiritual motherhood of Mary unites us in a special way in the all-embracing solidarity of salvation — the bearing of one another's burdens — that has its source, center, and summit in Jesus Christ. We rightly venerate Mary as the Mother of the Church. And we honor her truly when we live as fully as possible the saving event, bearing the burden of one another, praying and suffering that, finally, all may be one in the love of God.

We thank you, heavenly Father,
  that you have given us everything
in Jesus Christ, your only begotten Son,
  our Mediator and Savior.
And we thank you
  that you have given him Mary
  as the deaconess of salvation,
  the new Eve,
the mother of the living.
Our hearts are filled with gratitude
that you have given her to us
  in a unique spiritual motherhood.
May your Holy Spirit come upon us
that, with Mary, we may live in the unity
  of faith, hope, and love
and bear fruit for the life of the world.


O Mary, Mother of God, our mother,
pray for us now and at the hour of our death
that we may always praise your Son,
  Jesus Christ,
for his salvation of mankind
and thus be freed from perdition
  and the fear of death. Amen.

29

*Mary's Easter Joy*

"Early on the Sunday morning, while it was still dark, Mary of Magdala came to the tomb. She saw that the stone had been moved away from the entrance, and she ran to Simon Peter and the other disciple, the one whom Jesus loved. 'They have taken the Lord out of the tomb,' she cried, 'and we do not know where they have laid him.' So Peter and the other set out and made their way to the tomb. They were running side by side, but the other disciple outran Peter and reached the tomb first. He peered in and saw the linen wrappings lying there, but did not enter. Presently, Simon Peter came along behind him, and he went into the tomb. He saw the linen wrappings lying, and the napkin which had been over the head — not lying with the wrappings but rolled together in a place by itself. Then the disciple who had reached the tomb first went in too, and he saw and believed" (Jn 20:1-8).

On Easter morning, we find Peter with John the disciple to whom Mary had been entrusted. Did Mary know the two apostles were together? We might well think that she herself had encouraged the beloved disciple to look for Peter, knowing the abyss of his sadness and depression. With faith very much like Mary's, John, the virginal disciple of Christ, is "the man waiting for the coming of the Lord" and so he cares for the needs of his neighbor. He who had taken Mary into his home shares her maternal care for all, but in particular for those who have a special mission in the Church.

I frequently ask myself how it is possible that the texts of the Gospel mention the Easter faith of so many others and not that of Mary, the Mother of Jesus. The response might be the following: The Gospels underline two aspects: first, the belief that Christ is truly risen and that he has revealed himself; and second, that the disciples came only gradually to the fullness of belief. Mary had fully lived the exodus with her Son, Jesus; she shared the depth of his mystery with him. She therefore was not faced with the difficulty which Peter, Mary Magdalene, and the disciples of Emmaus had in coming to a belief in Resurrection. She, our spiritual mother, is the model of the Easter faith of the whole Church. Intimately united with the suffering and death of Jesus, she is equally united with the joy of his Resurrection. *The closer we imitate her, the greater will be our Easter joy* and the simpler our path to fullness of faith.

The Gospel presents us with a number of other women who, even before the apostles, came to faith in Jesus Christ. John, the beloved disciple of Jesus, to whom Mary is entrusted, pays particular attention to Mary Magdalene's path of faith. She too, in her own way, is a model of our faith insofar as our faith needs further purification, greater clarity and strength. Mary Magdalene seeks and finds Jesus because of her great love, although the full light of faith does not break through at once. Both Mary, the Mother of Jesus, and Mary Magdalene should be subjects of our meditation: the innocent faith of maturity on one hand and, on the other, faith still in need of search and purification.

Easter day in the Gospel emphasizes the role of woman. Mary the Queen of the apostles is *the* woman. She is the one who with all her being sings the song of the Servant and the joy of the Resurrection. At her side are other women, who in the depth of their faith aid in the apostolic work of the Twelve. And, we can never forget that at the heart of the Church there are with Mary all those who believe in the risen Lord and spread this faith with all their being.

**We thank you, Father,**
 **for the gift of faith and the Easter joy**
**which you have first given to Mary,**
 **the Mother of Jesus,**
**then to John, the beloved disciple,**
**to Mary Magdalene and to many others**
 **including ourselves.**
**May we race along the path of faith like John,**
**and search for you with great love**
 **as Mary Magdalene did,**
**and find, with all our hearts and minds,**
 **Jesus, who reveals to us**
 **the depth of your love.**

Lord, grant us a humble, grateful,
   and joyous faith.

O Mary, blessed are you
for you have believed
that God's promise will be fulfilled.
Blessed are you in your Easter joy,
rejoicing in the faith of the apostles
and in the faith of so many humble people.
Pray for us that we seek first of all
   a living, grateful faith,
a faith that bears fruit
   in love and justice
for the salvation of the world,
a faith that brings all
   to know Jesus Christ,
the Son of the living God,
whom we have the honor to call your Son.
   Amen.

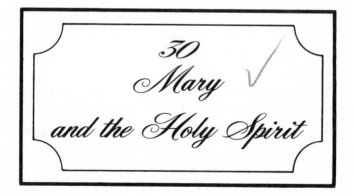

30
Mary
and the Holy Spirit

"Then they returned to Jerusalem. . . . Entering the city, they went to the room upstairs where they were lodging: Peter and John and James and Andrew, Philip and Thomas, Bartholomew and Matthew, James, son of Alphaeus and Simon the Zealot, and Judas, son of James. All these were constantly at prayer together, and with them a group of women, including Mary the mother of Jesus, and his brothers" (Acts 1:12-14).

Jesus' Mother, Mary, who since the great moment of redemption has also become the mother of John and of us all, is with the apostles at the great event of Pentecost. She lives her role in the new family of God represented by the apostles and the holy women and some of her relatives who followed her in faith. Her prayer and her presence among the apostles is essential for the preparation of the Pentecostal event. Mary, who is full of grace and totally guided by the Spirit, is indispensable for our life of prayer and our path to faith. The powerful coming of the Holy Spirit is prepared by the prayer and expectation of Mary and of the whole community with her.

"And they were all filled with the Holy Spirit" (Acts 2:4). It is the power of the Holy Spirit which gives full life to the Church of the paschal faith in a new Pentecost. The Church clearly refers to the importance of Mary's faith in the Nicene Creed: "We believe in the Holy Spirit, the Lord, the giver of Life. . . . He has spoken through the prophets." In a special way then, he speaks through Mary, the Queen of the prophets. Openness to the Spirit is always a gift of Christ, the new Adam; it can therefore never be separated from Mary's role as the new Eve, the mother of the living.

Mary, virgin and mother, first experienced the power of the Holy Spirit when she conceived the Word Incarnate in her womb. She became the model of faith through the grace of the same Holy Spirit. More than all the others, she experienced the Easter joy as a gift of the Spirit; and now she is fully at home with the new family of Jesus when they are filled with the Holy Spirit. Even more than the apostle Paul, can she exultantly say, "Thanks be to God . . . for in Christ Jesus, the life-giving law of the Spirit has set us free from the law of sin and death" (Rom 7:25; 8:2).

Mary was never under the law of sin. In God's design, and in her existence from beginning to end, she lives the new law of mutual love that comes from Christ who is the Covenant of the people. She has no reason to fear death. Death will be for her the final homecoming into the glory of her Son. She lives fully and knows the liberating law of the Spirit that unites her with Jesus who is the Christ, the One anointed by the Holy Spirit.

Mary, more than all the others saved by Jesus Christ, bears the fruit of the Spirit. "The harvest of the Spirit is love, joy, peace, patience, kindness, goodness, fidelity, gentleness and self-control" (Gal 5:22).

Mary, the spouse of the Holy Spirit, continuously invites the whole Church and each of us to an intensive life of prayer, to trust in the Lord, to praise and give thanks, and thus be faithful to the Covenant. An authentic devotion to Mary goes hand in hand with a confirmed faith in the Holy Spirit and an increasing docility toward his grace. Whoever loves and venerates Mary and adores the Holy Spirit with her cannot live like a slave under the law. Such a one will be able to live the new law that is manifested in the Eucharist and will *consider the gifts of the Holy Spirit together with the needs of fellow-men as the highest law.* This belongs to the very essence of the new birth in Christ and the ongoing spiritual renewal of the Church. We shall never be able to see the hoped-for new Pentecost of the Church — which John XXIII desired so earnestly — unless we nourish a deep love and veneration for Mary who teaches us how the whole Church can become a house of prayer, and how we all can learn to become adorers of God in spirit and truth.

We thank you, heavenly Father,
   for having given us Mary
as the model of fidelity
   to the law of the Spirit,
of joyous faith and firm commitment
   to the Messianic peace.
May your Holy Spirit come upon us
   abundantly
and so transform us that we too
   may bear fruit in justice,
in love, joy, peace, goodness,
   and gentleness
for the life of the world.


O Mary, you were the heart
   of the Church
when the apostles awaited
and experienced
the powerful coming of the Holy Spirit.
Pray for us that we may ever more

completely understand and experience
what it means to believe
in the Holy Spirit
and to adore him together with the Father
and the Son. Amen.

31
Mary,
Glorious in Heaven

"A great sign appeared in heaven, a woman robed with the sun — beneath her feet, the moon, at her head a crown of twelve stars. She was pregnant, and in the anguish of her labor, she cried out to be delivered. Then a second sign appeared in heaven: a great red dragon with seven heads and ten horns; on his head were seven diadems, and with his tail, he swept down a third of the stars in the sky and flung them to the earth. The dragon stood in front of the woman who was about to give birth so that when her child was born, he might devour it. She gave birth to a male child, who is destined to rule all nations with an iron rod. But her child was caught up to God and his throne; and the woman herself fled into the wilds, where she had a place prepared for her by God, there to be sustained for twelve hundred and sixty days.

"Then war broke out in heaven. Michael and his angels waged war upon the dragon. The dragon and his angels fought, but they had not the strength to win, and no foothold was left them in heaven. So the great dragon was thrown down, that serpent of old that led the whole world astray, whose name is Satan, or the devil — thrown down to the earth, and his angels with him.

"Then I heard a voice in heaven proclaiming aloud: 'This is the hour of victory for our God, the hour of his sovereignty and power, when his Christ comes to his rightful rule. For the accuser of our brothers is overthrown who day and night accused them before our God. By the sacrifice of the Lamb, they have conquered him, and by the testimony which they uttered; for they did not hold their lives too dear to lay them down. Rejoice then, you heavens and you who dwell in them.'

"When the dragon found that he had been thrown down to the earth, he went in pursuit of the woman who had given birth to the male child. But the woman was given two great eagle's wings to fly to the place in the wilds where for three years and a half, she was to be sustained, out of reach of the serpent" (Rv 12:1-14).

This Biblical text is somehow a synthesis of all that the Bible has said about Mary. She is presented again as the *woman,* the mother of the living, the new Eve. She is the Queen of the prophets who lives with intensity the joys, the hopes, and the anguish of her people. She is a prophetic sign. This whole text refers at the same time to Mary, the Mother of Jesus, and to the Church. We cannot understand the motherhood of the Church without that of Mary.

The prophetic vision of the Old Testament is accentuated here. "The kings of the earth set themselves, and the rulers take counsel together against the Lord and his anointed. . . . I will tell of the decree of the Lord. He said to me, 'You are my son; today I have begotten you. Ask of me, and I will make the nations your heritage' " (Ps 2:2-8). Most evident is the reference to the great vision of the Book of Genesis about the woman associated with the victory over Satan: "I will put enmity between you and the woman, and between your seed and her seed" (Gn 3:15). Mary, who so intensely lived these events, is always present to the Church whose whole history is marked by the same suffering, the same battle, the same hope and victory.

The "anguish of her labor" is not just a matter of the physical pangs of childbirth. It includes all the suffering Mary endured with hope as she gave birth to Jesus in the extremes of poverty, the flight into Eygpt, and all the other experiences of the new exodus — even unto the birth of the Church when Christ her Son died on the Cross to send us the Spirit. And together with John, the seer of Patmos, we view the Church, the new Sion, the mother of the living, who constantly gives birth to new sons and daughters, not without participating in the pangs of Mary's childbirth. Before her, the Church sees her children threatened by the inimical powers which try to devour them as soon as they come to spiritual birth.

"The woman herself fled into the wilds." The prophetic vision of the Book of Revelation reminds us of the flight of the Holy Family into Egypt as a real and prophetic symbol of how God deals with his Church. Again and again, he takes her into the wilds. She has to become pure; she is to renounce all earthly securities, all direct and indirect power over the temporal sphere. She cannot share in the final victory of Christ without constantly living the exodus which Jesus has lived with Mary.

"Her child was caught up to God and his throne." The almighty Father saved Jesus from the hands of Herod and freed him from the power of death in the paschal victory; as risen Lord, Jesus is living witness to the Father's glory. And we see now the humble woman whose life is a song — the song of the servant who has been raised up to glory. The daughter of Sion is the Queen of the apostles: the 12 stars indicate the new family of God represented by the 12 apostles. Her assumption into heaven, her life of glory with her Son, Jesus Christ, are divine promises to the Church that all the People of God will be exalted if they live fully as servants with Christ the Servant, following the example of Mary.

The whole vision of John reechoes the Magnificat: "The arrogant of heart and mind he has put to rout; he has brought down monarchs from their thrones, but the humble have been lifted high" (Lk 1:51-52). All the People of God should continually meditate on how Mary, together with Jesus, experienced the tremendous tension and struggle between two totally opposed Messianic expectations. Mary is the leader of those who know that the Messiah is the Servant of God and that only those can share in his final victory who are willing to follow him humbly in the poverty that is a gift of the Holy Spirit. The exact opposite of this poverty is any type of religion that seeks not to serve but to lord it over others. Jesus has come to drive out this devil: "Begone, Satan."

John, the beloved disciple to whom Mary is entrusted in a particular way, speaks here to the Church and announces salvation to her as long as she follows Christ the Servant with his Mother. The Church has no reason to fear insecurity or the pilgrimage through the desert as long as she *puts all her trust in the Lord.* The assumption of Mary into the glory of her Son is an encouragement to the Church to live the detachment, the poverty of the Spirit, and the humility of the servant.

It is impossible to overlook the reality of this great vision. In this historical hour, the Church is again urged by the Lord to live the advent and the exodus-hope. And she will live it with the prophetic prayer: "Maranatha: Come, Lord Jesus."

We thank you, Father,
    Lord of heaven and earth,
that you have given your Church
    the wonderful vision of John,
the beloved disciple.
Grant that we
    may ever better know the Church
as she is prefigured in Mary,

the humble handmaid,
the Queen of the apostles.
Send us your Holy Spirit
that we may know Christ,
and in him know you and your design
for the Church and the world,
and thus share in your life with your Son
in the Holy Spirit.

O Mary, Queen of the prophets, new Eve,
mother of the living,
protect, with your prayer and blessing,
the Church of your Son, Jesus Christ.
Pray for us that we may put all our trust
in Jesus Christ
who is your Son and whom you adore
as the Son of God,
our Lord, our Savior and our hope. Amen.